James Spencer Northcote

Epitaphs of the Catacombs

Christian Inscriptions in Rome during the first four Centuries

James Spencer Northcote

Epitaphs of the Catacombs
Christian Inscriptions in Rome during the first four Centuries

ISBN/EAN: 9783337330941

Printed in Europe, USA, Canada, Australia, Japan

Cover: Foto ©Lupo / pixelio.de

More available books at **www.hansebooks.com**

PREFACE.

When Mr. Brownlow and myself published our work on the Roman Catacombs in 1869, we apologised for the omission of all that concerned their inscriptions. We said that justice could not be done to this important branch of the subject until the second volume of De Rossi's "Inscriptiones Christianæ" should have been published. At the same time it was intimated that a volume was already in course of preparation, which was intended to introduce to the English reading public the principal results of his labours in the field of Christian epigraphy.

We have now a second edition of our "Roma Sotterranea" nearly ready, and the question necessarily arose whether the inscriptions should be again omitted. Nearly ten years have elapsed, and De Rossi's second volume has not appeared. On the other hand, it was found that the materials already collected were abundantly sufficient to fill a volume, and to give (it is believed) a very fair idea of the whole subject. I began to make a collection of Christian inscriptions in Rome in 1848, copying them both from books and from the stones themselves. In the present volume, however, I have trusted more to De Rossi's printed copies than to my own MSS., having learnt by long experience to have entire confidence in their accuracy. Most of the inscriptions, therefore, now presented to the public are taken from one or other of De Rossi's great works, viz., the first volume of the "Inscriptiones Christianæ," the three volumes of "Roma Sotterranea," or the fifteen volumes of his "Bullettino di Archeologia Cristiana." Great pains have been taken to reproduce them exactly as they are; and it has not been thought necessary to call attention to the faults of spelling or grammar where they are such as most readers will be able to correct for themselves.

This volume is published separately, for the convenience of possessors of the first edition of our "Roma Sotterranea" who might not care to purchase the much larger work just now going to the press. The matter, however, has been of course arranged with a view to the new edition, and thus a few pages will be found here that have been printed before.

J. S. N.

EASTER TUESDAY, 1878,
ST. MARY CHURCH, TORQUAY.

CONTENTS.

CHAPTER I.

INTRODUCTORY.

Universal use of epitaphs; their purpose; their brevity; usefulness and interest—Number of ancient Christian epitaphs known; not a seventh part of what once existed—Causes of their destruction in ancient, mediæval, and modern times—Dispersion of those which were preserved, in churches, convents, museums—Existing collections in Rome—Action of the Popes with reference to them—The plan of a Lapidarian Gallery projected, lost sight of, and at last badly executed—Christian Museum at the Lateran projected by Gregory XVI., and executed by Pius IX.—The inscriptions there, whence obtained by De Rossi; how arranged—Importance of this sketch—Roman inscriptions copied by scholars of the eighth and ninth, fourteenth and fifteenth centuries—Other collections by Bosio, Fabretti, Boldetti, Marangoni, and others—De Rossi undertakes to publish a complete collection—First volume appears in 1864—Its contents arranged not topographically, nor theologically, but chronologically, ... 1

CHAPTER II.

A VISIT TO THE LATERAN MUSEUM.

Some general features of the inscriptions collected there—(1.) Different style of engraving; some excellent, some very bad, executed by unprofessional hands; some only painted; several in the Catacombs scratched in the mortar—(2.) Mixture of languages, even on Pagan monuments—The use of Greek ordinarily a token of antiquity—(3.) Corrupt forms of spelling—(4.) The presence of the letters D.M.—(5.) Minute measurement of length of life—General arrangement of the inscriptions—Columns I.-III. Public sacred inscriptions—IV.-VII. Chronological—XVIII.-XXIV. Topographical—XXI.-XXIV. Not from the Roman Catacombs—XVIII. Of single names only, and painted, not engraved, from St. Priscilla—XX. Quite in classical style, from Cœmeterium Ostrianum—XIX. All Greek, from Prætextatus, . . . 17

CHAPTER III.

CHRONOLOGY OF THE INSCRIPTIONS.

Proportions of dated and undated inscriptions of first six centuries—Their chronological distribution—Present book confined to first four centuries—Dated inscriptions extraordinarily rare during this period—Mode of distinguishing undated inscriptions—Two great classes of Christian epitaphs known by certain tokens—In the most ancient, no note of length of life or day of death, but ancient symbols, Greek language, short pious acclamations, special phrases—In the later class, laudatory epithets of deceased; other special phrases; monograms, crosses, &c.—Reasons of this difference—Its reality proved by examples—Another point of difference in names—Occasional exceptions—Other differences determined by geographical, not chronological, limits—Examples—Importtant results obtained by observing these distinctions, . . 37

CHAPTER IV.

PAGAN EPITAPHS.

Necessity of studying Pagan epitaphs—Points of contrast—To Pagans, death was without hope; an eternal farewell—Yet imaginary exchange of salutations between the living and the dead—Sepulchres—Sententiæ sepulchrales on the vanity of life expressed

Contents.

under a variety of images—Different views taken of life; sensual, practical, trifling, enigmatical, serious—Testimony given by the epitaphs to the state of domestic life in Rome—Strong expressions of natural affection—Parents and children—Impatience at untimely death—Husbands and wives—Some titles of praise or affection perhaps only conventional—Yet the facts recorded are true and very creditable—Domestic virtues praised in women, . 58

CHAPTER V.

THE TEACHING OF CHRISTIAN EPITAPHS ABOUT DEATH AND THE DEAD.

Contrast between Pagan and Christian epitaphs—Christian epigraphy perfected by degrees, but its general character shown from the first; simple, hopeful, and joyous; less religious in the fourth and later centuries—Life and love, characteristics of the most ancient epitaphs—Some exceptions, chiefly of later date—An episcopal instruction on death in the third century—Language of epitaphs denotes belief in future resurrection—Acclamations for the dead; of life in God, peace, refreshment—These phrases and some others explained—The same prayers found in the Liturgies, ancient and modern—Prayers addressed to the dead by surviving friends and relatives—Religious character of these prayers, and their orthodoxy, ... 73

CHAPTER VI.

DOGMATIC ALLUSIONS.

Unreasonable to look for an exposition of Christian doctrine in epitaphs, yet some allusions to it may be expected—This expectation realised with reference to belief in one God, in Christ, and in the Holy Ghost—Some peculiar phrases with reference to the Holy Trinity—Devotion to the Saints, ... 97

CHAPTER VII.

THEIR TESTIMONY TO CERTAIN POINTS OF DISCIPLINE AND PRACTICE.

PAGE

Evidence from the inscriptions of the Catacombs to—(1.) The hierarchy, pope, bishop, priest, deacon, exorcist, lector, fossor or ostiarius—(2.) Widows and virgins—(3.) The laity, fideles, fratres, neophytes, catechumens—(4.) The sacraments of baptism, confirmation, and Holy Eucharist, ... 110

CHAPTER VIII.

THEIR MORAL AND SOCIAL ASPECT.

Interest of ancient inscriptions as records of mere human thought and feeling—Special interest of ancient Christian epitaphs—Acts of the Martyrs, the only other records of the same period—Importance of these two witnesses when they agree, *e.g.*, in omitting all mention of titles, parentage, country—Of slaves; freedmen; alumni; love of the poor; of labour; of chastity; innocence—Practical conclusions, ... 138

CHAPTER IX.

INSCRIPTIONS WITH SYMBOLS.

Epitaphs with symbolical ornamentation—Three classes of symbols—I. Religious: The Good Shepherd, Noe's ark, dove, fish, anchor, peacock, lighthouse, crowns, horse, cross, monogram in varieties of form, crux gammata—II. Civil: Marble cutters, carpenter, blacksmith, fisherman, dentist, surgeon, soldier; III. Nominal: Pagan as well as Christian examples, . . . 155

CHAPTER X.

CONCLUSION.

Inscriptions of Pope Damasus—Chief characteristics of Christian epitaphs, their hopefulness—They reflect contemporary history and general state of Christian thought and feeling at different periods—Ancient Christian epitaphs in other countries; Great Britain, Spain, and Gaul—Conclusion, ... 176

INDEX of Greek Names and Words, . 189

INDEX of Latin Names and Words, . . 190

INDEX of English Names and Words, . 194

EXPLANATION OF MARGINAL REFERENCES., &c.

R.S. . . . . . De Rossi's Roma Sotterranea.
I.C. . . . . .   ,,   Inscriptiones Christianæ.
Bull. . . . .   ,,   Bullettino di Archeologia Cristiana.
C.I.L. . . . Corpus Inscriptionum Latinarum. In course of publication by the Academy of Berlin.
O.H. . . . . Inscriptionum Latinarum Selectarum Amplissima Collectio. Edited by Orelli; with a third volume, edited by Henzen.
I.R.N. . . . . Inscriptiones Regni Neapolitani. Edited by Theodore Mommsen.
L.B. . . . . . Inscriptions Chrétiennes de la Gaule. Edited by M. E. Le Blant.

EPITAPHS OF THE CATACOMBS.

CHAPTER I.

INTRODUCTORY.

Universal use of epitaphs; their purpose; their brevity; usefulness and interest—Number of ancient Christian epitaphs known; not a seventh part of what once existed—Causes of their destruction in ancient, mediæval, and modern times—Dispersion of those which were preserved, in churches, convents, museums—Existing collections in Rome—Action of the Popes with reference to them—The plan of a Lapidarian Gallery projected, lost sight of, and at last badly executed—Christian Museum at the Lateran projected by Gregory XVI., and executed by Pius IX. —The inscriptions there, whence obtained by De Rossi; how arranged —Importance of this sketch—Roman inscriptions copied by scholars of the eighth and ninth, fourteenth and fifteenth centuries—Other collections by Bosio, Fabretti, Boldetti, Marangoni, and others—De Rossi undertakes to publish a complete collection—First volume appears in 1864—Its contents arranged not topographically, nor theologically, but chronologically.

FROM the earliest ages, and in all stages of civilisation, men have sought to preserve their memories from decay by means of inscriptions, more particularly by inscriptions graven upon their tombs; as though they would fain bid special defiance to the envious tooth of Time there where its bite seemed to be at once inevitable and fatal. In one inscription, this "last writing" is spoken of as a certain "solace in death, as by it is preserved the eternal recollection of one's name and family;" and in another, set up by a sorrowing widow, we read, "Although a hard lot has taken away my

_{Universal use of epitaphs.}

_{O.II., 7408. 7405.}

husband's life, yet, so long as this inscription shall last, the memory of his praise and glory shall remain for ever. Aurelia Sabina to my dearest, sweetest, most affectionate, and incomparable husband, with whom I lived without any quarrelling (*lesione animi*) for twenty years and two months." And the common preface to so many of these inscriptions, ÆTERNÆ MEMORIÆ, testify to the same truth, viz., that they were dictated by a desire to keep alive, as long as might be, the memory of the deceased.

Their purpose,

Under these circumstances, it is not to be wondered at that such stones are, as Orelli pathetically laments, "rarely very communicative." It often happens that they provoke rather than satisfy curiosity; they might have told us so much more that it would have been interesting to know, but which we now seek in vain to elicit from their laconic brevity. The author of the *Religio Medici* expresses his disappointment that they "deliver precisely the extent of men's lives, but seldom the manner of their deaths, which history itself so often leaves obscure in the records of memorable persons." But we are not all members of the Royal College of Physicians; and there are other points of view besides the medical from which epitaphs may be studied, and their brevity regretted. However, in spite of their brevity, they have often furnished important contributions to our stores of historical knowledge, and sometimes also in other branches of human science they have rendered valuable services. And independently of these accidental uses which may occasionally be made of them, there is another and a more general interest which almost always attaches to them, if only they contain something more than a name and a date—the interest, namely, which belongs to the records of human thought and feeling under circumstances which are common to us all, viz., the thought of death, as anticipated by ourselves or already suffered by our friends and relatives; the general view taken of life now that it is over; the feelings of regret at the loss of friends; the good qualities selected for commendation in the

brevity,

usefulness and interest.

Introductory. 3

notice of the deceased, and the way in which the love or respect of the survivors is testified. We have most of us, at some time or other of our lives, beguiled an idle hour by spelling out the monuments of some village churchyard with reference to these and similar particulars, and have rarely failed to derive amusement or instruction from the occupation. The same fruits may of course be gathered from the study of collections of monumental inscriptions, whether brought together in museums or copied into books; and if the collection be sufficiently large, and tolerably homogeneous, they often teach us more of the inner life, give us a more lively picture of the temper and mode of thought which characterised the people to whom they belong, than the more elaborate productions of their poets, philosophers, or historians.

Of Christian inscriptions in Rome during the first six centuries, De Rossi has studied more than fifteen thousand, the immense majority of which were taken from the Catacombs; and he tells us that there is still an average yearly addition of about five hundred derived from the same source. This number, vast as it is, is but a poor remnant of what once existed. From the collections made in the eighth and ninth centuries, it appears that there were once at least 170 ancient Christian inscriptions in Rome which had an historical or monumental character; written generally in metre, and to be seen at that time in the places they were intended to illustrate. Of these, only 26 remain, either whole or in parts. In the Roman topographies of the seventh century, 140 sepulchres of famous martyrs and confessors are enumerated: we have recovered only twenty inscribed memorials to assist us in the identification of these. Only nine epitaphs have come to light belonging to the bishops of Rome during these same six centuries; and yet, during that period, there were certainly buried in the suburbs of the city upwards of sixty. Thus, whatever facts we take as the basis of our calculation, it would seem that scarcely a seventh part of the original wealth of the Roman Church in memorials of this

[margin: Number of ancient Christian epitaphs known.]

[margin: Not a seventh part of what once existed.]

kind has survived the wreck of ages; and De Rossi gives it as his conviction that there were once more than 100,000 of them.

Causes of their destruction in ancient,

There is evidence in the history of the Catacombs that the work of destruction began in very early times; and that the Popes did what they could to supply the loss.[1] The invasions of Alaric in 410, of Genseric in 455, Ricimer in 472, Vitiges in 537, and (worst of all) Totila in 546, all did something towards destroying the monuments of ancient Christianity in Rome. Probably the Lombards in 754 did still more; but we are afraid that by far the greatest amount of loss cannot be set down to the account of ancient barbarians and enemies, but has been due to the carelessness or want of judgment of friends, and in comparatively modern times. Pope Paul I., and the other Pontiffs who followed his example, seem only to have translated the relics from the Catacombs, but to have left inscribed tombstones where they were. But there is good

mediæval,

reason to believe that from the eleventh to the fifteenth century, whilst the Catacombs lay buried in darkness, large numbers of these stones were used, not only in Rome, but even in distant places, for the pavements of churches. The shape and the thinness of these slabs of marble recommended them as specially suitable for that kind of tesselated pavement improperly called *opus Alexandrinum*, which was just then in fashion; and it seems certain from the numerous fragments which remain, that Roman masons used them freely for this purpose, both in the

Bull., 1875, pp. 111-131.

Lateran Basilica within the walls, and in churches at Genazzano, Corneto, and elsewhere. De Rossi suggests, in extenuation of the fault, that perhaps there was an idea of fitness in using in sacred places stones that were already in a manner sacred. However, by and by came the Renaissance, and in some instances these tesselated pavements were destroyed to make room for newer fashions; and the stones perished with them: even where they were retained, it soon became impossible to

---

[1] See inscription in Lateran Museum, iii. 6.

Introductory. 5

decipher the inscriptions, cut up into many fragments, and worn away by the continual treading of many people.

Even when the Catacombs were rediscovered (in 1578), and their importance recognised, this portion of their contents hardly fared better than before. Churches in Rome and Naples, Rocca di Papa, Anagni, Velletri, and hundreds upon hundreds of private chapels in different parts of the world, received these stones either for their pavements, as before, or for the ornamentation of their porticoes or sacristies, or to be placed in museums as interesting relics of Christian antiquity. Some private individuals, also, and religious communities, took pleasure in collecting and preserving them in the walls of their houses and cloisters. The museums which had been formed before this time had not cared to possess such things. On the contrary, they were rigorously excluded as rude and unclassical in style. Out of fourteen or fifteen Lapidarian collections which De Rossi can trace as having been made in the palaces or villas of learned Romans between the middle of the fifteenth and the middle of the sixteenth century, only three had any Christian inscriptions at all; and these only one in each. Even in two of these instances it would seem to have been admitted by an oversight, since there is nothing remarkable in either of them; and the third had been selected apparently because of the beauty and accuracy with which the letters were engraved, and because of the monogram which stood at the head of it.

and modern times. Dispersion of those which were preserved, in churches, convents,

But after the days of Bosio a more Christian taste began to prevail, and De Rossi is able to enumerate some twenty or more Italian nobles, besides ecclesiastical dignitaries and religious communities, who interested themselves in making a collection of inscriptions and other objects from the Catacombs. Of course very many of these private collections have suffered the usual fate of such things; they have been sold and dispersed on the death of the collector, or some change in the circumstances or tastes of the family. Those that were made by

and museums.

6 Epitaphs of the Catacombs.

Existing collections in Rome.

religious bodies have not suffered in this way, *e.g.*, that of the Jesuits in the Kircherian Museum at the Roman College; those of the Benedictines at St. Paul's in Rome and St. Peter's in Perugia; those of the Camaldolese at St. Gregory's on Monte Celio, and of the Canons Regular at St. Agnes' and St. Laurence's, both *fuori le mura*.

Action of the Popes with reference to them.

After all, however, these collections are very limited in extent, and quite unequal to the greatness and importance of the subject. Nothing really worthy could be hoped for unless the Sovereign Pontiffs could be persuaded to take the matter in hand, and carry it through to a successful issue. It had engaged the attention of several of them at various times from the middle of the fifteenth century. Pope Nicholas V., A.D. 1447, seems to have entertained the idea of collecting all the Lapidarian monuments of early Christianity which were at that time known to exist; and both Eugenius IV., his immediate predecessor, and Calixtus III., who succeeded him, and Sixtus IV., a few years later, A.D. 1471, forbade, under heavy penalties, the alienation or destruction of anything belonging to this class of monuments. When Leo X., too, appointed Raphael to superintend the works at the rebuilding of St. Peter's, he gave him a special charge that the *res lapidaria* should not be injured. In later times, these injunctions became more earnest and more frequent in proportion to the increasing number and importance of the inscriptions that were brought to light. Still nothing practical appears to have been devised until the reign of Clement XI., when Boldetti proposed that collections of

The plan of a Lapidarian Gallery projected;

Pagan and Christian inscriptions should be arranged opposite to one another on the walls of the long gallery which leads to the Vatican Library and Museum. The learned prelate Francesco Bianchini supported this recommendation, and it was cordially approved by the Pope. The unhappy circumstances of the times, however, prevented him from carrying it out.

After the lapse of another half century, learned men pressed upon Benedict XIV., A.D. 1750, the foundation of a Christian

Museum, in the interests not only of learning but of religion; lost sight of; and the work was at last taken in hand, but not wisely conducted. A hall was selected in the Vatican Library, and it was determined to arrange along its walls as many of the ancient Christian sarcophagi as could be brought together. Many were bought from private individuals into whose possession they had passed; others were removed from public places where they had been used for fountains and other profane purposes. Unhappily, however, they were not left in their integrity. For economy of space, the *bassi-rilievi* were first sawn off from the monuments to which they belonged, and then, for symmetry's sake, parts of different sculptures were put together to fill up the allotted space, and even parts added or taken away that they might fit exactly the Procrustean measure. As to the inscriptions, the Bishop of Anagni was called upon to supply an inventory of all that Marangoni had sent to that city, A.D. 1720-40, as though there were an intention of requiring restitution of them; but this intention, if ever entertained, was certainly not fulfilled. A few only were taken up from the pavement of the Churches of Sta. Maria in Trastevere and San Martino ai Monti in Rome; and these, together with others then recently extracted from the Catacombs, were arranged above the cornice of the Library.

Thus Boldetti's excellent idea of forming a grand Lapidarian Gallery, where the contrast between Pagan and Christian epitaphs might be conveniently studied, seemed to have been altogether lost sight of, whilst its execution became day by day more difficult. At last, in the beginning of this century, Pius VII. intrusted the work to the celebrated scholar Gaetano Marini. Under his direction, four or five private collections were bought; other specimens were purchased from the dealers in such articles; and to these were added all the recent acquisitions from the Catacombs, until about 1100 had been brought together. Marini, however, took no pains to make the most even of the paltry amount of materials thus collected. Whilst and at last badly executed.

distributing the Pagan inscriptions into various classes, he merely inserted the Christian monuments into the wall, without giving any indication where they had been found, or making any attempts to classify them, beyond separating the few which contain the names of the Consuls from those which are without this chronological note. His work, therefore, left much to desire, both on account of its defective arrangement and its narrow limits. And already during the reign of Gregory XVI. there was talk of a Christian Museum at the Lateran under the superintendence of Father Marchi. The space, however, devoted to the Gregorian Museum proved to be too small for the purpose; it was soon entirely filled with monuments of classical antiquity, so that it was reserved for our late Holy Father, Pope Pius IX., to found another Museum there, which should be exclusively Christian. To Father Marchi was intrusted the collection and arrangement of all monuments of painting or sculpture; to De Rossi all that concerned Christian epigraphy.

Christian Museum at the Lateran projected by Gregory XVI.;

and executed by Pius IX.

The bulk of the materials placed at De Rossi's disposal were inscriptions that had been accumulated during the last thirty years and more in the storerooms of the Vatican Library; others were contributed by the Municipality from the storerooms of the Capitoline Museum; others were recovered from the chapels and sacristies of convents, where some of them had been hidden out of sight for nearly two hundred years; the few that had been placed over the cornice of the Vatican Library by Benedict XIV. were transferred, and a selection made from those which Marini had placed in the Lapidarian Gallery; finally, plaster casts were taken of others which it was not desirable to move from the sites with which they were historically associated. A considerable number of inscriptions having thus been brought together, it became necessary to fix upon some principle of classification. Chronology and topography obviously suggested two such principles, each very valuable in its way, yet neither of them on the whole satisfactory. Chronology was precisely the point which had hitherto been too much neglected; it was still

The inscriptions there, whence obtained by De Rossi;

and how arranged.

the most difficult and tedious part of De Rossi's daily archæological labours. The time was not yet come when a true and certain chronology of the subterranean cemeteries had been established; still less had definite chronological canons as to the monuments which they contain been sufficiently discussed, defined, and accepted by the learned. Any chronological arrangement, therefore, that might have been attempted would have seemed arbitrary, and could only be justified by long dissertations in books, not *primâ facie* by the inscriptions themselves. Nor would a topographical arrangement have fared better. The precise spot where each inscription had been found was often enveloped in much obscurity; and, moreover, since many of the subterranean cemeteries had been in use contemporaneously, a merely topographical arrangement would have involved many useless repetitions, and led to no satisfactory results. It was determined, therefore, to arrange them mainly according to the sense or contents of the inscriptions, without altogether excluding, however, as we shall presently see, the other principles of division, both chronological and topographical.

We have entered thus minutely into the history of the formation of these various collections of Christian inscriptions, because ignorance of it has led some writers into grave errors. They have spoken of the Lapidarian Gallery at the Vatican, for example, as though it were a selection of the most ancient, curious, and valuable specimens of Christian epigraphy, "made under Papal superintendence," and therefore (as they did not hesitate to say) not made in a spirit of loyal devotion to the truth, but in obedience to the exigencies of theological controversy; whereas, as we have shown, it was really no selection at all. The only selection that has ever been made under this condition is that of which we have just spoken at the Lateran; and even this was no selection from the entire treasures of antiquity, but only from the fragments that could be recovered after the long-continued plunder of a wreck. That this figure is no exaggeration, the

Importance of this sketch.

history we have given sufficiently proves. The number of ancient epitaphs actually in existence is quite insignificant when compared with those which have been destroyed or lost. However, small as it is, the Lateran selection is very interesting, and it belongs to our subject to give some account of it.

Roman inscriptions copied

But, first, we must say a few words about other collections of Christian inscriptions that are to be found not in museums but in libraries; that is to say, not of the original stones, but of written or printed copies of their contents.

by scholars

There is no evidence of any scholar having devoted his attention to this subject before the days of Charlemagne. But in the intellectual movement which characterised that age, some of Alcuin's scholars were careful to copy inscriptions which they saw in the course of their travels, especially those on public monuments in Rome. They made their selection, however, not so much in the interests either of archæology or of history, as for purely literary purposes. They gave the preference to inscriptions that were written in verse, and (as it would seem) they aimed chiefly at making a collection of *formulæ*, which they might imitate in their own compositions. Hence they omitted to specify all those particulars which are most essential to their value in the eyes of an archæologist or historian, such as their date, their authorship, their precise locality. We are sure of this, because in some few instances the stones which they copied still exist, and we find on them the very particulars we were in want of, but which had not been inserted in the MS. copies.

of the eighth and ninth centuries,

C.I.L., vi. p. 9.

The oldest collection of this kind now known was made by some visitor to Rome in the eighth or ninth century, who returned to Switzerland by way of Ticino, and probably took his MS. home with him to some monastery of which he was a member in that country. It was once in the library of the monastery of Pfeffers, and is now at Einseidlen. The whole collection does not exceed eighty, and about a third of them are Christian. It was first published by Mabillon in 1685, and has been quite recently republished by the Berlin Academy as a fitting introduction to their "*Inscriptiones Urbis Romæ Latinæ.*" Other collections were made about the same time and under similar circumstances; that is to say, they were made by Northern scholars visiting Rome, and anxious to carry home with them some of the literary wealth with which they found that city so abundantly stored. At least, this seems to be the most probable account that can be given of them; and hence it is that no vestige of such MSS. has ever been found in the libraries of Italy, but only in Germany, France, and Switzerland; and it is conjectured that similar treasures may yet lie hid in some of the libraries of our own country.

During the fourteenth and fifteenth centuries many such collections were made, both by Italian and German scholars; for the most part, however, they were of Heathen inscriptions only, or, if any of Christian origin were admitted, they were both few in number, and not in any way distinguished from the more numerous memorials of Paganism. The first distinct collection of *Christian* inscriptions was made towards the very close of the fifteenth century by one Petrus Sabinus, a Professor of Humanities in the Roman University, and a friend and fellow academician of Pomponius Letus. They were about 200 in number, collected (he tells us) with great diligence from the marble slabs or the mosaics of the Roman churches; and even these formed an appendix to a much larger collection of Pagan inscriptions. It is only in our own day, and by the indefatigable perseverance of De Rossi, that this work, written in 1495, and dedicated to Charles VIII. of France, then making his triumphal progress through Italy, has been discovered in St. Mark's Library, at Venice.

and of the fourteenth and fifteenth.

Sabinus was followed by many others of more or less distinction, who were probably incited to undertake the labour of collecting the memorials of past ages by seeing the work of destruction, the burning of libraries, the sacking and pulling down of churches, that was then going on by the soldiers of the

Emperor Charles V. It is not worth while to enumerate the names of these collectors, since they preceded the discovery of the Catacombs, and cannot therefore be said even to have laid the foundation of those works which have succeeded that event. It will be sufficient to observe, that though they admitted into their pages inscriptions of comparatively recent date, yet the whole number thus preserved to us falls short of a thousand.

Other collections by Bosio, Fabretti, Boldetti, Marangoni, and others.

Bosio made a most careful collection of all the inscriptions he found in the Catacombs, and seems to have intended to publish them in a separate volume; dying, however, before any of his works had been printed, Severano, to whom his papers were confided, followed a different arrangement, and the epitaphs appeared as an appendix to the account of each cemetery in which they had been discovered. Fabretti, Boldetti, and Marangoni (all of them officially connected with subterranean Rome, and the two last having devoted nearly forty years to its study) made considerable additions to this collection; unhappily, however, they did not imitate the minute care and accuracy of their predecessor, so that their copies of inscriptions cannot be altogether depended upon. Lupi, Buonarroti, Bottari, Zaccaria, and a host of other names now crowd upon us, each making contributions, more or less valuable, to the *res epigraphica* of ancient Christendom.

But such a multitude of materials, dispersed in fragments over so many different volumes, and receiving fresh additions almost daily from the excavations always being continued in the Catacombs, required to be brought together into one body and to be carefully and judiciously arranged. It was a gigantic work, demanding immense industry and perseverance, great tact also and skill in arrangement; moreover, the undivided attention of a sufficiently long life. No wonder, then, that though many conceived the idea of undertaking it, yet all failed: to some was wanting patience; to others, a well-digested plan; to all, time; and the only result of all these abortive efforts has been a number of voluminous MSS. in the Vatican and

Introductory.

other libraries, and of incomplete works in the world at large. The history of all these failures must have suggested discouraging thoughts to De Rossi as he recorded them in the preface to his own collection, in which he undertakes to publish all the Christian inscriptions of Rome during the first six centuries. And indeed, when we think of the shortness of human life, the immense extent of the work to be accomplished, and the scrupulous exactness without which De Rossi will not be content to publish, we feel many misgivings lest the same fate should await him also, and the magnificent volume he has published remain always an *opus imperfectum*. He had begun to apply himself to the work in the year 1842; in 1844, Father Marchi published an announcement to this effect, without the knowledge of the author. In 1846, the very year of his accession, Pope Pius IX. declared his intention of adopting the work as a public undertaking, and defraying its expenses. It was then hoped that the publication would begin in the course of three or four years, but it was delayed by various causes, both private and public, till 1857, and the first volume did not really appear until the year 1864. Fourteen more years have passed, and we are still without the second volume. We believe that it is ready, or very nearly ready, for the press; but the property of the Camera Apostolica, which published the first volume, having passed into the hands of the Italian Government, political complications now add their quota to the many hindrances of the work. All who have at heart the interests either of learning or religion—for it is of very great importance to both— must sincerely hope that these obstacles may be soon removed. Meanwhile, we have reason to be thankful for the instalment already received; for this first volume contains what may be called the framework or skeleton into which all other parts must ultimately be fitted. It deals with the driest, most difficult, and yet most important part of the subject—we mean the chronology; and it deals with it in a way which has commanded the approbation of all competent judges.

Marginal notes: De Rossi undertakes to publish a complete collection. First volume appears in 1864. Its contents arranged, *not topo-graphically,*

In modern times, it seems to be acknowledged that, as a general rule, a topographical arrangement of inscriptions is the most scientific and convenient. It has the advantage of enabling the reader to distinguish local peculiarities from universal practice; moreover, it facilitates the work of interpretation, and enables us to complete fragmentary portions of history with greater accuracy. And though De Rossi's inscriptions came all from one place, Rome and its neighbourhood (within a radius of thirty miles, more or less), yet he himself too considers this topographical arrangement so important, that he will adopt it as far as he can, *i.e.*, he will assign all the epitaphs which he publishes to the several Catacombs or other cemeteries whence they were originally taken. But if he had made this the only principle of his arrangement, he would have risked the loss of that which to most persons will be the chief value of the collection, viz., the light which it will throw upon the doctrines, the discipline, and temper of mind of the early Church. For each inscription, taken by itself, is so short and simple, that it scarcely seems adequate perhaps for the illustration of anything. It is only when all these feeble rays of light are gathered together and concentrated in one focus that they can be shown to be of any real value.

nor theologically,

But neither again, on the other hand, could he adopt a theological arrangement, such as had been proposed by Zaccaria and partially carried out by Marini; otherwise he would certainly have made shipwreck of his labour from another cause. For inscriptions are only valuable as testimonies to matters of fact and history when their own antiquity has been first demonstrated. And if this is true of inscriptions generally, how much more so of these, against which so formidable an amount of theological prejudice was sure to be arrayed the moment they were brought into court.

but chronologically.

De Rossi, therefore, with excellent judgment, has devoted his first volume to a chronological arrangement of his treasures, or at least of a portion of his treasures; that portion, namely,

Introductory. 15

which bears its exact age stamped upon it. Not a single inscription among the fourteen or fifteen hundred here presented to the public but bears the name of some Consul, or other historical or chronological note whereby it can be assigned with certainty either to this or that year in particular, or to one of two, three, or half a dozen years, to which the same notes belong indifferently. Some of the inscriptions may or may not be interesting and important from another point of view, historical, philological, or theological; it matters not; they receive no favour on that account in the volume of which we are speaking. They may have very important evidence to give by and by, but the time is not yet come for this. For the present, each witness, as he comes into court, is questioned and cross-questioned very closely as to his age, and then is relentlessly set aside, to be recalled perhaps on some future occasion. "I fear," says the author, in the first chapter of his Prolegomena, *I.C.*, i. p. 1. "that lovers of Christian antiquity, as soon as they have dipped into this volume, and seen that scarcely anything is explained in it but the lists of Consuls, the cycles of the sun and moon, and other chronological items of this sort (whereas they were anxiously looking for some illustration of the history, the dogmas, or the rites and ceremonies of the Christian Church), will feel themselves grievously disappointed and deceived. Perhaps, also, impatient of the tedious length and difficulties of this circuitous route, they will highly disapprove and condemn my whole plan. Such persons I certainly would not persuade to weary and disgust themselves by a diligent study of these pages; I feel keenly, and frankly acknowledge, that only a few, initiated as it were into the mysteries of the science of epigraphy, will be able to derive either pleasure or profit from their perusal. Let others, then, be content, if they will, with running through it in the most cursory manner, or let them leave it alone altogether, unless they happen to light on something which arrests their attention, and seems to them worth examining. Doubtless this is a painful fact, and much to be regretted, and most assuredly none regrets it more than myself. There is nothing I would more anxiously desire than that the fruits of my labour should be at once appreciated and enjoyed by many persons; it would be much more to my taste to gratify the desire of the multitude than to provide for the learned few. Nevertheless, I had rather adopt a plan that shall be solid and true than one which is only tempting in appearance. I hold the substantial benefits that are to be derived from this science to be infinitely more important than mere show and display: and I have resolved on beginning my vast work in this way, because I know of no other whereby I can lay good solid foundations, sufficient to bear the weight of the building which I mean to raise on it. For there is nothing that people are more anxious for in this matter, nothing that they are wont more eagerly to demand of me, than that I should, first of all, establish with certainty the dates of all the monuments I produce. Without this, they are either useless, or, at best, of very slight and doubtful use, for the elucidation of Christian antiquity."[1]

[1] The historical sketch in the early part of this chapter is taken from a "Memoria" on the "Museo Epigrafico Cristiano Pio-Lateranense," written by De Rossi, and presented with photographic plates of the whole collection to Pope Pius IX. on the occasion of his episcopal jubilee in 1877.

CHAPTER II.

A VISIT TO THE LATERAN MUSEUM.

Some general features of the inscriptions collected there—(1.) *Different style of engraving; some excellent, some very bad, executed by unprofessional hands; some only painted; several in the Catacombs scratched in the mortar—*(2.) *Mixture of languages, even on Pagan monuments—The use of Greek ordinarily a token of antiquity—*(3.) *Corrupt forms of spelling—*(4.) *The presence of the letters D.M.—*(5.) *Minute measurement of length of life—General arrangement of the inscriptions—Columns I.-III. Public sacred inscriptions—IV.-VII. Chronological—XVIII.-XXIV. Topographical—XXI.-XXIV. Not from the Roman Catacombs—XVIII. Of single names only, and painted, not engraved, from St. Priscilla—XX. Quite in classical style, from Cœmeterium Ostrianum—XIX. All Greek, from Prætextatus.*

THE first step towards a practical introduction to the study of Christian epigraphy should be a visit to the Christian Museum at the Lateran, and a careful inspection of the inscriptions that are collected there. We have seen how this collection was formed; let us now take at least a cursory view of its contents. We shall have occasion to return to some parts of it again, but it will be useful to gain some general notions about the whole before we enter on any detailed examination of its parts.

Some general features of the inscriptions collected in the Lateran Museum.

The feature which will probably be the first to strike most persons inspecting these epitaphs is the great diversity of style in their execution. This varies from some of the most beautiful specimens of monumental engraving which could be desired, e.g., in Columns I. and III., to the most wretched and illegible scribbling. Of course this is not to be wondered at. There would have been different degrees of rank and wealth,

(1.) Different style of engraving; some excellent, some very bad, executed by unprofessional hands.

of skill, taste, talent, and education among the ancient Christians as amongst ourselves; and this inequality would have been reflected in this as in a thousand other ways. It is not, however, the superior excellence of some specimens which strikes us so much, as the extreme badness of others; and the explanation of this seems to be, that the work was often done not by professional hands or with proper instruments, but rudely and hurriedly scratched with the sharp edge of the trowel, or even with a nail, by some sorrowing survivor when he revisited the grave, or, more frequently, as he still lingered by its side after the funeral service was over. In some, and these the most ancient, the letters are not cut at all, but only written upon the surface in red or black paint. The inscriptions on the famous tombs of the Scipios were originally written only in this way (in red), and so also the inscriptions in some of the Etruscan sepulchres. And Mommsen says that the fashion of incising the epitaphs came from Greece.

Some only painted.

C.I.L., i. p. 11.

Several in the Catacombs scratched in the mortar.

In the Catacombs there were other inscriptions of a still more primitive simplicity, merely traced in the fresh mortar with which the gravestones were secured. These, of course, could not be transferred to the museum. Many have been wholly or partially destroyed by the opening of the tombs which they had once been intended to identify. Several, however, still remain in their places, looking as fresh and perfect as though they had been made but yesterday. The visitor to the Catacombs should not fail to notice them; *e.g.*, in the Cemetery of St. Agnes, near the old entrance to it, *Abundantia in pace Tur...antia in pace Kal Junii Nepotiano et Facundo Coss, i.e.,* June 1st, A.D. 336.

(2.) Mixture of languages.

The next point which arrests the student's attention as he walks through the gallery at the Lateran is the curious mixture of languages which these epitaphs exhibit. In some instances Latin and Greek are mingled in the strangest confusion; the epitaph begins perhaps in one language and ends in another; or, still more frequently, the Latin language is used, but the

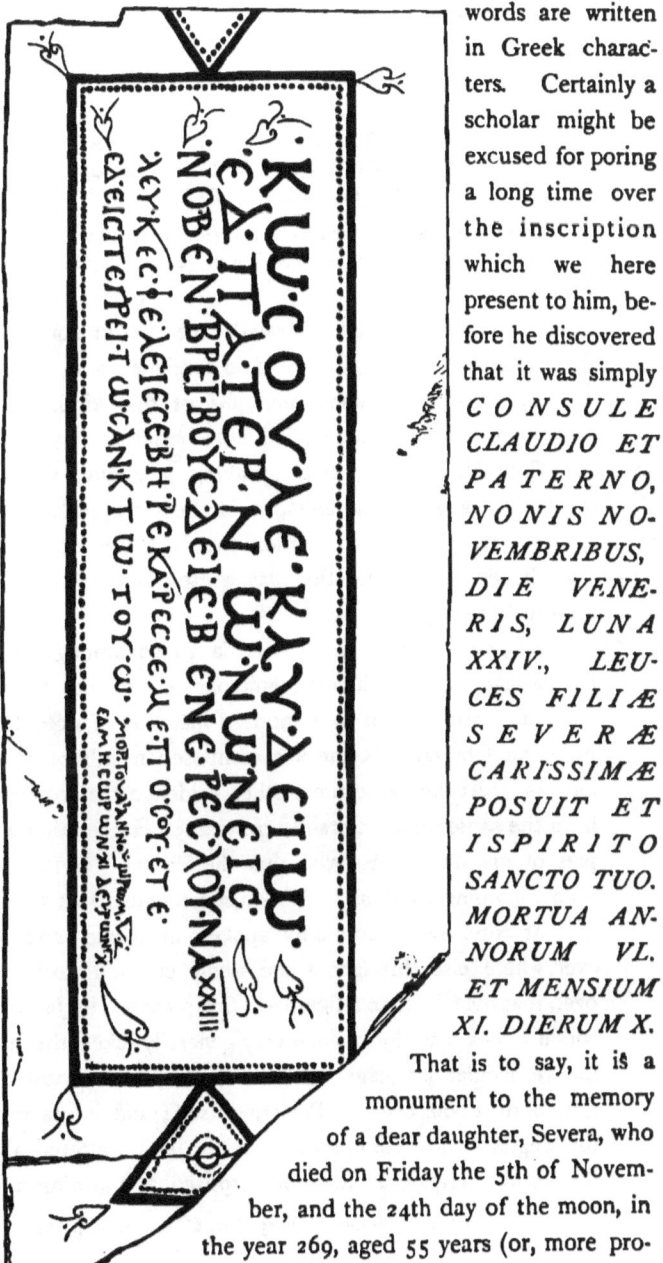

words are written in Greek characters. Certainly a scholar might be excused for poring a long time over the inscription which we here present to him, before he discovered that it was simply *CONSULE CLAUDIO ET PATERNO, NONIS NOVEMBRIBUS, DIE VENERIS, LUNA XXIV., LEUCES FILIÆ SEVERÆ CARISSIMÆ POSUIT ET ISPIRITO SANCTO TUO. MORTUA ANNORUM VL. ET MENSIUM XI. DIERUM X.*

That is to say, it is a monument to the memory of a dear daughter, Severa, who died on Friday the 5th of November, and the 24th day of the moon, in the year 269, aged 55 years (or, more probably, 6), 11 months, and 10 days.

We will add another specimen, much more beautifully engraved, belonging to the year 345; it is all written in Greek letters, but the first line only is of Greek words, the other two of Latin—

CΩΚΡΑΤΗC ΑΕΙΜΝΗCΤΟC ΦΙΛΟ [θεος]
ΔΗΠΟCΕΙΤΟVC Θ Κ ΩΚΤΒ ΑΜ [αντω]
ΑΝΝΟVC ΤΡΙΓΙΝΤΑ ΙΝ ΠΑΚΕ.

"Socrates, ever to be remembered, beloved by God, buried on the 23d of September, when Amantius was Consul (A.D. 345). He lived thirty years. In peace."

In a future chapter we shall see reason for believing that this was the epitaph of a foreigner who had died in Rome; and occasional epitaphs of this kind, belonging to strangers, are of course liable to recur at any period of the Church's history; but, speaking generally, the use of the Greek language on epitaphs of the Catacombs is a note of antiquity. De Rossi considers that it creates a presumption that the epitaph in question was written before the middle of the third century.

The use of Greek ordinarily a token of antiquity.
Bull., 1865, p. 52.

This prevalence of the Greek language among the more ancient families of Christian epitaphs falls in with the theory so much insisted upon by a modern historian of note, that the primitive Church at Rome was composed mainly of Jews and Greeks.[1] At the same time, other evidence that comes to us from the same source certainly convicts of exaggeration another part of his statements—viz., that the Church "contained few, if any, genuine Romans." We must remember that Greek was at that time very commonly spoken in Rome, and indeed everywhere else throughout the whole civilised world; moreover, that the Christian religion was first preached by Jews, among whom Greek had long since very generally taken the place of the vernacular language. It was spoken, and almost universally understood, even in Palestine itself; and it was certainly the language most common among the Jews scattered all over the world. Hence we are not surprised at the almost entire

[1] St. Paul in Rome, by Very Rev. C. Merivale, p. 36.

absence of the Hebrew language from the epitaphs in the Catacombs (only a single example, we believe, having yet been found), nor at the prevalence of the Greek.

We shall see in the course of this chapter specimens of a large class of epitaphs from one of the subterranean cemeteries, written with very great elegance, both in Greek characters and in the Greek language; and inscriptions of the same kind are to be found in the more ancient parts of several others—*e.g.*, on a stone of unusual size, closing a grave of the second century in the Cemetery of Domitilla, we read:—

ΦΛ CABEINOC KAI
TITIANH AΔEΛΦOL

Bull., 1875, p. 65. *Tav.*, v. 4.

"Flavius Sabinus and Titiana, brother and sister."

The use of the characters of one language to express the words of another, which we saw in the two previous examples, must be attributed to the carelessness or ignorance of the engraver, who perhaps was hardly conscious what language he was using. This at least is the supposition of Mommsen with regard to a similar anomaly to be observed on some sepulchral inscriptions in Etruria. In the most ancient tombs of that country the name of the deceased was written or engraved in the Etruscan language; but in proportion as the use of the Latin tongue spread throughout the country, a number of hybrid *tituli* were made of Etruscan words written in Latin characters, or of Latin with traces of the Etruscan language corrupting them. Even among the Pagan monuments in Rome there are not wanting examples of Latin words written in Greek characters, *e.g.*, ΣΕCΣTOC KΛΛΔIOC, ANTI ΔION TEPTION, &c.; and they are very frequent on the walls of Pompeii.

C.I.L., i. p. 254.

C.I.L., i. p. 212.

Even on Pagan monuments.

Another point of interest to a scholar, as he runs his eye over these ancient monuments, will be various corrupt forms of spelling, partaking for the most part of a phonetic character, and foreshadowing in some particulars the formation of modern

(3.) Corrupt forms of spelling.

Italian. We will only mention two, which are perhaps the most prominent. The first is the frequent disuse of the final consonant, especially in the case of pronouns, the names of numbers, and other words in very common use, such as *septe, nove, dece*, &c. And the second is the prefix of a vowel to facilitate the pronunciation of an initial *s* before a consonant, as *ispiritus* for *spiritus*, of which we have already seen an example in page 19, and which is to be noticed universally in the Latin inscriptions of Spain.

<small>C.I.L., ii. p. 395.</small>

<small>(4.) The presence of the letters D.M.</small>

Looking more closely at the substance of the inscriptions in the Lateran, the student cannot fail to have his attention arrested by the appearance of the letters D.M. or D.M.S. engraved at the head of some few of them. If he is a novice in the study, he will be startled by this trace of Heathenism on Christian monuments; or, if the fact is not new to him, he will probably be aware that some authors have endeavoured to build a theory upon it as to the joint use of the Catacombs as places of burial by Pagans and Christians promiscuously. In either case, they require a word of explanation. The truth is, that out of fifteen thousand ancient Christian inscriptions, the obnoxious letters do not occur upon more than forty, *i.e.*, on one out of 375, whereas upon the Pagan epitaphs of the same period they are found on 95 out of a hundred. The letters only came into fashion on Pagan tombstones under the earlier Cæsars; but in process of time they became so common as to be looked upon as the distinctive marks of a mortuary inscription, and were doubtless engraved beforehand on tombstones kept ready for sale. In this way we account for finding them at the beginning of a Greek inscription in Pisa, and on what seems to have been the gravestone of a Jew in Rome. Of course, it is quite possible that in the same way some careless or ill-instructed Christians may have used them without taking heed to their presence, or even understanding their meaning. Sometimes there is evidence of an attempt on the part of the Christian to erase the objectionable title; some-

<small>Very rare.</small>

<small>C.I.L., ii. 463.</small>

<small>O.H., 4720.</small>
<small>How explained. R.S., i. 343.</small>

<small>Bull., 1865, p. 40.</small>

A Visit to the Lateran Museum. 23

times it is Christianised by the insertion of the sacred mono- *Bull.*, 1873, gram of Christ between the D.M. and the S, or by its addition $_{L.M., \text{viii. 7.}}^{\text{p. 129.}}$ both before and after the title; and this has been found on inscriptions in Sardinia, France, Greece, and Syria.

It is remarkable that in several instances the apparently Pagan title is followed by more than usually unequivocal tokens of the Christian faith, *e.g.* :— *I.C.*, No. 1192.

D. M.
LEOPARDUS QUI VIXIT [ANNOS]
ET MENSES N. XI. R S S[ANCTUM]
ELATUS EST VIII. IDUS AUG.
AUG.

We do not know the exact date of this, but the phrase "gave back his holy spirit" (*reddidit spiritum sanctum*) sounds older than the fourth century, so does the classical word *elatus* for "buried." On the other hand, the letters are never found on the oldest Christian epitaphs, but generally on those later than the middle of the third century. De Rossi thinks it probable that they were sometimes intended to stand for *Dignæ* or *Dulci Memoriæ*. He does not accept the suggestion of Boldetti, Fabretti, and others, that they were meant for *Deo Magno* or *Maximo*, excepting in such cases as have been mentioned, where they are united with the monogram. On the other hand, he would not willingly condemn the writers of these epitaphs of superstition and a voluntary adherence to Pagan errors, except upon irrefragable evidence; and this is certainly not forthcoming.

One of the most remarkable examples by which it is attempted Special to establish the charge of superstition is an inscription to be examined. seen in the Museum at the Capitol, a copy of which is also in the Lateran. It stands thus :—

D.M.A.   SACRUM XL. *L..M.*, ix. 32.
LEOPARDUM IN PACEM CUM SPIRITA SANTA ACCEP
TUM EUMTE ABEATIS INNOCINEM
POSUER. PAR. Q. AN. N. VII. MEN. VII.

Dr. McCaul[1] compares with this a heathen inscription in which a wife calls upon the Manes *commendatum habeatis meum conjugem;* and he concludes that "there can be no question that in the Christian inscription his parents asked the Pagan deities of the unseen world after death to receive with favour their innocent son." Now we cannot deny that at first sight there seems to be a certain close resemblance between the petition of this poor Pagan widow and that of the Christian parents of the boy Leopardus. Moreover, other Pagan epitaphs might have been quoted, in which the very same word "receive" is used as applied to the conduct of the Manes towards the dead. Nevertheless, it seems to us not only unnecessary, but even impossible, to accept Dr. McCaul's conclusion.

First of all, the letters of the title are confessedly uncommon, and very difficult of interpretation. We do not accept, any more than he does, Raoul Rochette's expansion of the formula into *Divis martyribus sacrum quadraginta*, because we know of no other example or authority for such a rendering; and therefore this suggested interpretation seems almost as daring as that of the good monk who insisted on interpreting the letters I.O.M. on an old stone over the doorway of his convent *Introitus omnium monachorum*, instead of *Jovi optimo maximo*. At the same time D.M.A. is a very unusual contraction for *Dis manibus*. We do not know of any other example. Of course, D.M.S. is the most common formula; in some places—*e.g.*, in Lyons and part of the Grisons territory—the S. is uniformly omitted. But there are occasional variations, such as in Spain, D.O.M., which Hubner would render *Dis omnibus manibus* (or *Deo optimo maximo*), refusing altogether to accept *Dis occultis manibus*, which some had suggested. On the other hand, he seems to admit *Dis inferis manibus* as the explanation of D.I.M. on an inscription in Lisbon, which Orelli rejects on a similar inscription in Perugia, preferring to see in the first

---

[1] Christian Epitaphs of the First Six Centuries, p. 61. London, Bell & Daldy.

two letters only an abbreviation of *Dis*. If this abbreviation be admitted, M.A. might in like manner be received as the substitute for *manibus*, as Dr. McCaul suggests, therein following the lead of Mabillon. We cannot propose any other reading which is more probable; but even so, there still remains an insoluble difficulty in the numeral XL.

Setting aside, then, for a moment the whole of the title as though it were not there, the epitaph begins, according to one of the most ancient Christian formulas, commending the deceased "to peace, in the company of the holy souls." Then, having these *spirita sancta* present to their minds, the parents go on (as it seems to us) to call upon them to receive their innocent son; finally, they add the usual particulars as to the length of his life. When we remember how frequently the writers of these epitaphs violate all laws of correct writing, and in the course of a few lines pass from the third person to the first without any warning, following the sequence of ideas rather than of grammar, it seems to us much more natural to suppose that the address was made to the holy souls than to the *Di manes* of the title, even without any reference to the theological aspect of the matter. And it is obvious to observe that it is thus brought into the strictest harmony with several other epitaphs which we shall have occasion to quote in a future chapter, but of which we may be allowed here to present a single specimen because of its great similarity to the epitaph under discussion:—

> PAULO FILIO MERENTI IN PA
> CEM TE SUSCIPIAN OMNIUM ISPIRI
> TA SANCTORUM QUI VIXIT ANNOS II. DIES N.L.

Bull., 1875, p. 19.

"To Paul, a well-deserving son, who lived two years and fifty days. May the spirits of all the saints receive thee into peace."

On the whole, then, we conclude that these forty examples of the letters of a Pagan formula inserted at the head of a Christian monument are too few in number and too doubtful in character to warrant the conclusions that have been sometimes drawn from them. There may have been carelessness in some instances, or real ignorance in others. Some may have even thought the use of them an indifferent matter, as the Christian Emperor who, at a much later period, did not hesitate to speak of tombs as *Ædificia Manium*;[1] others may have thought it convenient to retain them, though understanding by them very different words from those which the Pagans understood. We do not know of more than one Christian monument in which the words are inserted at full length, and not one which indulges in any of those addresses to the Manes which are not uncommon on Pagan monuments; as in the case of the widow already mentioned, who, after commending her husband to the good keeping of the spirits, prays them "to be indulgent to him, so that she may see him in the hours of night, and even to add her death to his, that so she may the more quickly and sweetly enjoy his company again."

(5.) Minute measurement of length of life,

Another peculiarity on some of these inscriptions which we think a scholar is likely to notice, is that the length of life is measured with an exactness quite unfamiliar to modern practice. It would have been less surprising if this had been confined to the epitaphs of children, but we find the mention of days, and even of fractions of days, in the case of lives which have been extended to fifty or sixty years. On a Pagan monument to a boy, the child of a slave born in the house, his mistress recorded of her "dearest *Verna*" that he had lived five years, two months, six days, and six hours; and that the accuracy of her arithmetic might be tested, she sets down the days of his birth and his death, which we see were both included in her calculation. In like manner, De Rossi gives us, from the Cemetery of St. Callixtus, the inscription of a Christian father to his son, "who had lived one year, three months, twenty-three days, six hours and a half. In peace." And we find another in the collection of Fabretti on which the reckoning is even

I.R.H., 3360. 3372.

O.H., 4341. 4718.

R.S., iii. xviii. 56.

Pp. 96, 219.

[1] Cod. Theod. IX., xvii. 4.

more minute, for it names four hours and six *scrupuli* or fifteen
minutes (a *scrupulus* being the twenty-fourth part of an hour).

In some instances the duration of married life is measured
with the same precision; as where a man puts up a *titulus* "to
his dearest wife, with whom I lived so many years"—the stone
is imperfect just where the number was inscribed—" six months,
three days, and fifteen hours." It is not easy to divine the
motive which dictated this epitaph, for the widower goes on to
say, " On the day of her death I gave the greatest thanks both
to gods and men" (*aput Deos et aput homines*). In another
instance, a wife burying her husband says she has lived with
him three years, two months, and eleven hours.

or of married life.

O.H., 4636.

4656.

Occasionally, not only the day but even the hour of birth
is mentioned, and not only the day of the month but the day
of the week. In some of these instances, De Rossi bids us
suspect a leaning on the part of the writers towards the mysteries
of astrology—*e.g.*, in a monument of the year 364, a child who
was born at the fourth hour of the night (it is not said on what
day) seems to have died " on Saturday, the 8th of May, on the
twentieth day of the moon, in the sign Capricorn;" and De
Rossi shows that each of these particulars was held in ancient
times to be unlucky. Another inscription tells of a boy, who
lived to be more than six years old, that he had been born at
the sixth hour of the night, on a Wednesday in the month of
May; died at the tenth hour on the 24th of June, and was
buried at the fourth hour—we presume on the following day,
as we gather from many inscriptions that this was the usual
practice—and that a large number attended his funeral (*elatus
est frequentia maximâ*). It is recorded on several of the later
inscriptions from the Cemetery of St. Callixtus on what day of
the week a child had been born or had died; and the days
are usually called by their Pagan names, *dies Solis, dies Mer-
curii, dies Veneris*, &c., just as they are called also in the writings of Justin Martyr, Clement of Alexandria, and others. But
in an inscription of the year 404, the 26th of June is called the

I.C., i. p. lxxxiv.
L.M., v. 6.

O.H., 4716.

R.S., iii. xviii.
29, 39; xx. 40.

Lord's Day, *dies Dominica*, and it can be proved by calculation that this fell in that year on Sunday.

I.C., i. No. 529.

Doubtless the profound student will find many more particulars in the inscriptions of this gallery which claim his attention, and even any educated man may feel his curiosity aroused by peculiarities of which he would desire an explanation. We cannot pretend, however, to enumerate them all. It must suffice to have noticed those which seem to us the most important or of the most frequent recurrence; and we trust that, with the assistance we offer, any intelligent visitor to the Lateran Museum will find there not a mere collection of stones, but a well-ordered book, open and easy to be understood by all who have a moderate knowledge of ancient times and the art of interpreting monuments. It remains, however, that we should give a few words of explanation as to the general principle of their arrangement.

General arrangement of the inscriptions.

The inscriptions are arranged in the walls of the open portico which runs round three sides of the first quadrangle of the palace on the first floor. The series begins with three columns of what De Rossi calls *sacred* inscriptions *par excellence*, because they were not primarily memorials of private individuals, as common epitaphs are, but they were either public monuments of the Christian religion, or they were inscriptions set up to the honour of individual martyrs. All these, from the necessity of the case, are of a comparatively late date; that is, they do not begin till the age of Constantine, and the *elogia* of the martyrs were the composition of Pope Damasus in the latter half of the fourth century. But all the other inscriptions collected here are epitaphs, and they are divided into three classes—the first and last chronological and topographical, the intermediate one arranged according to their contents. This class, by far the most numerous and the most interesting, ought not to be examined till after the others, as they can be made to furnish a sort of introduction to it,

Columns I.-III.

Public sacred inscriptions.

All the rest epitaphs.

supplying useful standards of comparison, and several important tests, both chronological and historical.

Of the first class, which fills Columns IV.-VII., we do not think it necessary to give any specimens. There are about 130 of them, out of the 1500 of the same class which either still exist or are known from authentic records to have existed; and their value consists in this, that they all bear the names of the Consuls or some other mark of time, which fixes their date. The whole class, of which they are a sample, occupies, as we have seen, the first volume of De Rossi's great work, which is intended to comprise all the Christian inscriptions of the first six centuries; and a study of that work is indispensable to those of our readers who desire to go deeply into the subject. *IV.-VII. Chronological.*

The earliest inscription in the volume and in the gallery belongs to the third year of Vespasian, or A.D. 71. Unhappily, it is a mere fragment that has survived, containing nothing more than the date. The second is of the year 238. It is written in Greek, and is interesting chiefly because of the unusual detail which is recorded of the number of days during which the deceased was ill;[1] the epithet also by which he is characterised, θεοφιλέστατος, or most beloved of God, is not so frequently met with as some others; and the overflowing tenderness of the bereaved father leads him to say of his child that he was "sweeter to him than light and life itself." The third, A.D. 273, is engraved on the lid of a sarcophagus, and was found in the cemetery of Prætextatus. It consists of a single name and the date of the death.

But it would take us too long to go through them all in detail; neither would the fruit of such an examination be at all in proportion to its labour. We shall confine ourselves therefore to the mention of a few particulars that are either specially interesting in themselves, or promise to be specially useful when we come to speak of the great mass of inscriptions

---

[1] Some persons understand the same detail to be recorded in an inscription of the year 370, No. 214 in De Rossi's volume.

that are undated; and we will take them indifferently from the Lateran Gallery or from De Rossi's printed volume, only taking care to specify the dates of the epitaphs to which we are indebted for them.

Characteristics of the more ancient symbols;

First, then, we observe the very ancient symbols of the fish and the anchor only on an epitaph of the year 234: the bird, with or without the olive branch, very frequently, especially in the latter half of the fourth century; there are ten or twelve examples between 346 and 408: the *orante* also, or figure of the deceased holding out his arms in prayer, appears during the same period, A.D. 375, 382, 403, and 409. The earliest example on these monuments of the monogram ☧ is in the year 331; it is engraved with the prefatory words *In signo* between two palm branches, after the age of the deceased and before the names of the Consuls. The addition of Alpha and Omega on either side of it are on stones of the years 362, 367, and 371. B.M. is found at the beginning of inscriptions in 336, 346, and 350, whilst in one of 343 the words stand at full length—*Bonæ Memoriæ.*

phrases.

The dead are spoken of as asleep in epitaphs of all ages—*e.g.*, 249, 311, 397; but the grave is spoken of as though it were man's last and eternal home (*domus æterna*) in inscriptions which are comparatively late, A.D. 356, 363 and 407. The phrase *In pace* appears in an epitaph A.D. 290; and after the middle of the next century is rarely absent; sometimes standing alone, sometimes coupled with the word used to denote the death or burial, or with the verb *quiescit.* The prayer "Mayest thou live among the saints" is found on an epitaph of A.D. 268 (or 279); and "Mayest thou be refreshed with the holy souls," in the year 291; and in the year 307, "Sweet soul, drink and live;" which is common enough on drinking cups, but is rarely found in epitaphs. After the conversion of Constantine there is no instance of these simple and affectionate prayers for the deceased. Once only, A.D. 380, we find a petition to the

A Visit to the Lateran Museum. 31

deceased that she will pray for the child she has left behind her.

The post-Constantinian inscriptions are for the most part purely historical or biographical in their substance. They record the length of life; probably also there is another record of the length of time during which the husband and wife lived together; sometimes also mention is made of the civil or ecclesiastical position of the deceased; and, finally, the day of death or of burial. In the case of wives and children, laudatory epithets, sometimes of an extravagant kind, are added from the middle of the fourth century. Wives are praised as of marvellous goodness and holiness, marvellous industry and goodness, marvellous integrity and prudence, of rare example, &c.; and children, even of four or five years of age, "of wonderful innocence and wisdom;" and one lady, named Rufina, aged twenty-one, is spoken of as though she were the very personification of all that was perfect, A.D. 381—"*Infantiæ ætas, virginitatis integritas, morum grabitas, fidei et reverentiæ disciplina hic sita Rufina jacet ætat. xxi.*" Lastly, there are two or three epitaphs where the praise is of a more distinctive character, or is expressed in a more striking way; as when the deceased is called "a lover of the poor," A.D. 341 and 377, or "friendly to all," A.D. 385; or where it is said of a wife that her industry and thriftiness (*conservantia*) could hardly be found in any one else, A.D. 379; or of a child who died before he was eighteen months old, A.D. 382 (whose panegyric was not improbably due to the same author as the preceding), that he was innocent and "*innocentium misericors;*" and then the father is made to indulge in the following outburst of his feelings, which sounds rather rhetorical than real—"Who has not lamented and poured forth affectionate tears for your age? My future hope was looked for in thee; by thee, by thee, O Celerinus, I looked for everlasting glory. Thou restest in peace." This is one of the very rare instances in which these ancient epitaphs indulge in any long expression of sentiment; and the reader

Characteristics of those after Constantine.

will observe that it was towards the latest period of the use of the Catacombs as places of burial. Those of Marius and Alexander, which are printed in some books as belonging to the ages of persecution, and in which the deceased are represented as lamenting over the hardness of the times in which they live, are not genuine.

<small>XVIII.-XXIV. Topographical.</small>

We shall have occasion to return to some of these again in a future chapter. At present we will pass on to Columns XVIII.-XXIV., of which we said that the inscriptions are arranged topographically. Of these, some lie outside our subject,

<small>XXI.-XXIV. not from the Roman Catacombs.</small>

e.g., Column XXI., on the score of place, because they come from Ostia; but we shall call our readers' attention to certain interesting peculiarities to be observed in these in a future chapter. The inscriptions in Column XXII. were discovered in 1842, in the cemetery near St. Peter's, of which Pope Damasus speaks in his verses on the Baptistery of that Basilica; but this cemetery was not subterranean. In like manner the inscriptions in Column XXIII. do not come from the Catacomb of Cyriaca, but from the cemetery which was made above that Catacomb; and those in Column XXIV. come from the sepulchres of the Basilica of St. Pancrazio, and are of the sixth century. There remain in this topographical division three columns, XVIII.-XX., all of which concern us much, as they contain samples of particular classes of inscriptions which are assigned to the most ancient dates. We have given on the next page a small selection from them.

The reader will see at a glance that not all belong to the same family. One feature they have in common—the absence of any but the most ancient emblems, the dove, the fish, the anchor and the palm branch; but there is a marked difference between the engraving of those at the top of the page and those

<small>XVIII. of single names only; painted, not engraved; from St. Priscilla.</small>

at the bottom. In fact, these last, 13-20, are not really engraved at all, but merely painted with red paint on the slabs of terra-cotta with which the graves in this part of the Catacomb of St. Priscilla are closed; and the three slabs of the last speci-

men were attached to the grave in wrong order. They should have stood, of course, PAX TECUM FILUMENA, as in 16, PAX TECUM URANIA, a phrase which is slightly altered in 19 to PAX TIBI; but the rest from this catacomb simply give the name of the deceased, either without any addition whatever, or with the addition only of the Christian emblem of hope, the anchor. This is on the epitaph of one whose name was Hope, *Elpis;* and there is a flavour of Christianity about the other names also in this category, Philumena, or Beloved; Felicitas, or Happiness; Urania, or Heavenly. Fortunata and Victorina also are among the rest which are to be seen in this column at the Lateran.

XX. quite in classical style, from Cæmeterium Ostrianum.

Those at the top of our page of illustrations (1-5) will attract attention from the beauty and boldness of their lettering, and the same characteristic belongs to all the forty which fill this column. They come from the Cœmeterium Ostrianum, which, in former years, was wont to be called the Catacomb of St. Agnes on the Via Nomentana, but which is in reality very much older than that saint, being the place in which, according to the Roman tradition, St. Peter himself baptized. We see here the three Roman names, or the two, according to classical usage; and the names themselves, and the forms of expression, are classical. On two of the specimens which we have selected the epithet given to the deceased is *dulcissimus;* on the column itself this epithet occurs a dozen times, and hardly any other; only ἀσύμητος once, and *innocens* once, both of which are, of course, to be found also on Pagan epitaphs. Tokens of Christianity, however, are not wanting. In our own selection one of the deceased is called "The little lamb of God;" to another are added the emblems of the fish and the anchor; and amongst those which our space would not allow us to copy are three or four more anchors, a dove, *In pace* half a dozen times, and once *Vivas in Deo.*

XIX. all Greek, from Prætextatus.

The middle of our page is taken up with seven epitaphs (6-12), which, with a single exception, are all Greek. They are a selection from Column XIX. of the Lateran, in which

A Visit to the Lateran Museum. 35

eight inscriptions may be seen in Latin as against twenty-one in Greek. They come from the most ancient part of the Cemetery of Prætextatus, and bear every mark of antiquity. The fish is found on one of them, the palm branch on another, the anchor on three, and the dove on four. Two names occur on several. The pious acclamation ZHCEC, "Mayest thou live," is the only addition made to the name in No. 10; the same occurs also in No. 6, to which is appended another acclamation at the end, "In God." "In peace" is written in its Greek form on No. 11. In the same epitaph the lady is described by two names, not as though they both belonged to her by the same legal right, as being her *nomen* and *prænomen*, but rather as though one were a familiar substitute for the other; "Agatha, who is also called Sirica." The same peculiarity may be observed in No. 6, "Hygeia, mayest thou live, with Stercorius who is also called Hyginus, in God." It was *Bull.*, 1866, common among all classes of Roman society in the second and p. 69. third centuries to have two personal names (*cognomina diacritica*), names arising partly from a popular origin or private usage in the family, partly from a real double cognomen of civil and legitimate use. They are generally coupled together by the formula *qui* (or *quæ*) *et*, and it is usual to put first the nickname or *sobriquet* (so to call it), the *signum* or *vocabulum*, as the Romans called it, and the true cognomen in the second *L.B.*, i. 75. place; but this order was sometimes reversed.

The contrast between the inscriptions in these three columns and those which bear their own dates in Columns IV.-VII. is too marked to escape the notice even of the most superficial observer. "It is easy to understand," says De Rossi, "even *Bull.*, 1877. *à priori* by the mere light of reason, how, from these special families of inscriptions, when studied collectively in groups, and examined in connection with the history of the places where they came, and their mutual relations both of resemblance and difference, their chronology stands forth clear and certain; not, of course, the precise years to which they severally belong, but at least the period." And so the two series of selected epitaphs which occupy the two lateral wings of the portico, the one arranged chronologically, the other topographically, when taken together, put into the hand of the student a most valuable clue whereby to distinguish the different ages of Christian epigraphy. And this distinction is essential to the right appreciation of the epitaphs which occupy the intervening columns (VIII.-XVI.); it is, in fact, the very basis of the science of Christian archæology. We must treat of it, therefore, at some length in a separate chapter.

CHAPTER III.

CHRONOLOGY OF THE INSCRIPTIONS.

Proportions of dated and undated inscriptions of first six centuries—Their chronological distribution—Present book confined to first four centuries—Dated inscriptions extraordinarily rare during this period—Mode of distinguishing undated inscriptions—Two great classes of Christian epitaphs known by certain tokens—In the most ancient no note of length of life or day of death, but ancient symbols, Greek language, short pious acclamations, special phrases—In the later class, laudatory epithets of deceased; other special phrases; monograms, crosses, &c.—Reasons of this difference—Its reality proved by examples—Another point of difference in names—Occasional exceptions—Other differences determined by geographical, not chronological, limits—Examples—Important results obtained by observing these distinctions.

IT has been mentioned that about fifteen thousand Christian inscriptions are known belonging to the first six centuries, and that about fifteen hundred of these are marked by dates which determine their chronology. It is to be observed, however, that these dated inscriptions are most unequally distributed in point of time. There is but one of the first century, two of the second, twenty-three or twenty-four of the third, five hundred (more or less) both of the fourth and of the fifth, and the remainder belong to the sixth. Thus nearly three-fourths of the dated inscriptions lie outside the scope of our present purpose, which is confined to the Christian epitaphs of the Catacombs, or at least of the period during which the Catacombs continued to be used for purposes of burial, *i.e.*, to the year A.D. 410.

For fifty or sixty years before that time, cemeteries of the ordinary kind had been made in Rome, that is to say, above ground; especially above the Catacombs and round the small

<small>Unequal distribution of dated inscriptions during first six centuries.</small>

<small>Very rare in first four.</small>

Basilicas which were connected with them. And during the changes and chances of more than a thousand years, some of the tombstones belonging to these upper cemeteries may have fallen through the *luminaria* into the lower. It is generally easy to distinguish the one set of inscriptions from the other by their different shape, size and bulk. But these differences do not concern us now. We propose to give an account of Christian epigraphy in Rome during the first four centuries, so far as it can be ascertained from both sources indifferently; and to help us to arrange them chronologically, we make our first appeal to those that bear their own dates on the face of them. Of these, we have less than thirty before the age of Constantine, barely ten of the reign of that Emperor, about seventy belonging to the reigns of his sons, a dozen or more of the reign of Julian, and not far short of three hundred belonging to the years which elapsed between the death of Julian and the capture of Rome by Alaric.

We next turn to the great bulk of the un-dated inscriptions, and ask to what epoch these ought to be referred. Are these also, like those with dates, to be divided mainly between the fourth, fifth, and sixth centuries, and only an insignificant fraction assigned to the earlier ages? or was the practice of adding the dates a fashion of late introduction?

Undated inscriptions very numerous, and generally ancient.

We know that it was the habit of the ancient Christians, as of the Pagans also, to mark the anniversaries of their departed friends by certain religious ceremonies; but at first they kept note of these days in their own private records, they did not inscribe them on the tombstones. Not only single inscriptions, but whole groups or families of inscriptions, which have been found under De Rossi's own eyes in parts of the Catacombs which he knows to have been most ancient, are uniformly without any such information. Those of the third century, he says, make more frequent mention of the day and month of the death (or burial), but even these, too, very rarely add the year; and the complete chronological formula, including the day, month, and year, becomes more and more common as we advance into the fourth century. If this be true, it follows that the great bulk of the Christian inscriptions of Rome are very ancient indeed; and it becomes a matter of the highest importance to find means of establishing, at least approximately, their date. How is this to be done?

The same problem often meets the student of Pagan monuments, and this is the way in which it is dealt with by Mommsen, who is generally admitted to be the most eminent authority on the subject. He says that as long as an inscription has to do with public events, it is manifestly possible in some degree to define its age, *e.g.*, it will rarely be difficult to distinguish a monument of the Republic from one of the Imperial period. But with private monuments, the case is different; only a few of these are dated, and their subject-matter is (generally) equally suitable to all ages. A genuine student, then, he says, will proceed in this way. He will first arrange all his examples before him, carefully eliminating all doubtful, corrupt, or false ones. He will then select those which have an epoch in any way defined, and from the certain will proceed to make out with some probability the age of the uncertain. He will mark all peculiarities of words or of spelling, *e.g.*, when certain phrases, at first confined to verse, came to be admitted into prose; when *ai* ceased to be written for *i*, *oe* for *u*, *quom* for *cum*, &c. By the time this collection and comparison of dated examples has been made, it will be found that many questions are solved. To attempt to solve them in any other way is to cut the knot with a leaden sword, a process which brings with it its own Nemesis for the blind impatience which prompted it.

De Rossi has followed precisely the course marked out by the great German critic; and those who have studied the volume he has published will often have had occasion to admire the patience and ingenuity with which his labours have been conducted, and the unexpectedly fruitful results by which they have been sometimes rewarded. But he has also derived

C.I.L., i. 204.

How to give the age of undated inscriptions.

Mommsen's method.

De Rossi's.

very valuable assistance, which is rarely within the reach of the collector of Pagan inscriptions, from a knowledge of the places where his monuments have been found. For by long observation his judgment as to the chronological order of development in the construction of the Catacombs has become extraordinarily sure and certain. We have ourselves known him correct, solely on this ground, the report of a date that was brought him by one who had seen the stone on which it was inscribed (in fact, who had helped to recover it from the *débris* under which it lay buried) in one of the galleries in the Cemetery of Prætextatus. De Rossi himself had not seen the stone, but he had formed his estimate of the date of that part of the Catacomb in which it was said to have been found; and he declared that the Consuls named to him belonged to a different period; his informant, therefore, must have either misread the names or misstated the site; and on proceeding to examine the inscription on the spot next morning, De Rossi proved to be right.

Moreover, it must not be forgotten, as a recent writer on history has well pointed out,[1] "that the great value of special training in any field of knowledge is to enable the inquirer to appreciate evidence inappreciable by mere common sense."

On every account, therefore, we have no hesitation in accepting De Rossi's assurance "that there are many tokens, such as the number and character of the names or of the symbols employed, the style of diction, the form of the letters, &c., which, if carefully examined and compared with one another, enable us not unfrequently to make a very probable statement as to the age of un-dated inscriptions (*probabili non raro sententiâ definies*); and that if, in addition to this, we know the place where the inscription was found, and have had the opportunity of examining other inscriptions from the same neighbourhood, it will rarely happen that there is any doubt at all about the age to which it belongs." It is not, of course, meant that it is possible to fix the year, or even the decade or score

I.C., i. 108.

---

[1] Mahaffy's Prolegomena to Ancient History, p. 76.

Chronology of the Inscriptions. 41

of years, perhaps; but De Rossi would certainly fix its chronology within the limits of half or quarter of a century (*tum de ætate late saltem sumptâ vix unquam grave dubium supererit*); he would never be in doubt with reference to any particular inscription, still less with reference to a whole class of inscriptions, whether it belonged to the ages of persecution or to the end of the fourth century.[1]

"There are two kinds of Christian inscriptions, very different from one another in diction and style. The main characteristic of the first is purity and simplicity; often the bare names and nothing else; no mention either of the age of the deceased, or of the day of his death, or of the person who set up the inscription. Often, however, symbols of various kinds, and especially those which had a secret Christian meaning, are added to inscriptions of this class, which are to be met with very abundantly in the most ancient parts of the Catacombs. The use of the Greek alphabet also is so frequent upon them that the Greek inscriptions sometimes equal, or even surpass, in number those which are written in Latin. Among epitaphs of this class others are very frequently mixed which exhibit, in addition to the names, short Greek or Latin acclamations, of great elegance, and with a savour of ancient simplicity about them, such as *Vivas in Deo, in Christo, in Domino, in pace, cum sanctis*, and the like; *Pete pro nobis, pro parentibus, pro conjuge, pro filiis, pro sorore; refrigera, in refrigerio, spiritum tuum Deus refrigeret, Deus tibi refrigeret*, and others of the same kind. Another particular worth mentioning about these ancient *formulæ* is that the souls of the deceased are not unfrequently called *spiritus sancti*.[2]

"There are some few epitaphs, however, which record the age of the deceased, the day of the death or burial (*depositio*), some

Two classes of Christian epitaphs.

In the most ancient no dates, but secret symbols.

Greek language.

Pious acclamations.

Special phrases.

---
[1] The importance of the subject must be our apology for continuing our quotation from De Rossi at some length, only occasionally abridging some of his arguments.
[2] Not a single instance of this occurs in the dated inscriptions after Constantine.

short praise of the deceased, and the names of those who put up the monument, and yet retain the phrases and sobriety, often even the elegance, of the old style. If I add that the writing and the diction of this early class of epitaphs often sins not only against elegance, but even against the laws of grammar, it will easily be understood that this must not be set down to the barbarism of the age, but to the unlettered condition of those who dictated them, and the genius of the vernacular language and pronunciation.

<small>In the latter class, date of death or burials.</small>

"The other kind of Christian inscriptions is as different as possible from the ancient simplicity, and all that savours of the vernacular. The families of inscriptions which belong to this class hardly ever omit to mention the length of the deceased's life, the day of his death, and especially of his burial, and all other particulars that are wont to belong to sepulchral inscriptions; and express these things by phrases and a certain

<small>Laudatory epithets.</small>

arrangement of words very different from the old style. They often begin with praises of the deceased, and this in bombastic and extravagant terms, *miræ sapientiæ, innocentiæ, sanctitatis;* also they continually denote the condition in life of the deceased, a thing which is very rarely indeed recorded in epitaphs of the older class. In some families of the later class of inscriptions, every specimen begins with such phrases as

<small>Special phrases.</small>

hic requiescit in pace, hic quiescit, hic jacet, hic positus est, which are almost always absent from inscriptions of the former kind. Lastly, almost every vestige is obliterated of those ancient acclamations which I have mentioned, and instead of them we have certain affected sentiments, expressed in cumbrous rhetorical form, almost worthy of the Iron Age. As to symbols, and especially such as conceal a hidden meaning, they are rarely to be met with; but in their place we have frequent

<small>Monograms, crosses, &c.</small>

representations of the monogram of Constantine, of the cross, and other signs òf the Church's triumph. This class of inscriptions is specially dominant in the cemeteries that were made in the open air; it is more rarely found in the subterranean

Chronology of the Inscriptions. 43

cemeteries or Catacombs, and only in those parts of them which are manifestly of most recent date.

"Everybody will at once understand from these tokens, that the style of epigraphy which characterises one of these classes of inscriptions belonged to the times when the Church was suffering persecution, and the other was the natural result of the peace and security which she afterwards enjoyed. For, as long as the Christian religion was proscribed by the Roman laws, and those who embraced it were liable to more or less bitter persecution, burying their dead deep in the bowels of the earth, and inscribing titles upon them which were never to see the light of day, they had scarcely any thought of handing down to posterity the memory either of men or of events. It was not for this purpose that they wrote epitaphs, but rather that they might satisfy their own sorrow and affection, and that, amid so many thousands of graves, each one might recognise that which was specially dear to him. For this reason it often happened that they did not even hand them over to professional hands for execution, but wrote them themselves either on the gravestone or on the mortar that secured it in its place. This accounts for their simplicity, for those touching phrases and acclamations so full of love and piety. When peace was given to the Church, and the triumph of the Christian faith was daily more and more secured, the opposite causes came into play; the style of epigraphy was necessarily changed; epitaphs began to be made either as private or public memorials, and in process of time, therefore, were marked with the date of the year.

Reasons of this difference.

"How complete a revolution was thereby wrought in the form and substance of Christian epitaphs, and how rapidly the old and beautiful style of acclamations fell into disuse, may be judged by an examination of all the inscriptions which are marked with dates, &c., published in this volume. Of these, there are about 1340 subsequent to the conversion of Constantine; and not one of them contains a single specimen of such acclamations, scarcely anything which even puts us in mind of

Reality of this difference proved by examples.

them. The only exceptions are the epitaph of Junius Bassus, of whom it is said that he went to God (*ivit ad Deum*), A.D. 359; of two children who died A.D. 431, of one of whom it is said that he "lived to God" fourteen years, and of the other that he was *petitus in pace* on the 11th of April; and of a lady who died on the 10th of June in the following year, and who is said to have been "received by God" (*accepta aput Deum*) on that day. Not one of the words *vivas, pete,* or *refrigera* occurs in any one of them; only once we find, on a fragment of an epitaph of unusual length belonging to the fifth century, the words *refrigeretur anima*. On the other hand, among thirty dated inscriptions prior to the conversion of Constantine, we have *receptus ad Deum*, A.D. 217; *vivas inter sanctos*, A.D. 268 (or 279); *filiæ carissimæ et spiritui sancto tuo*, A.D. 269; *refrigera cum spiritibus sanctis*, A.D. 291; *dulcis anima pie zeses*, A.D. 307; and *arcessitus ab angelis*, A.D. 310.

"Thus, then, whilst the very few inscriptions prior to Constantine which bear a consular date furnish us with striking examples of the characteristics of the more ancient style of Christian epigraphy, the far more numerous body of dated inscriptions of the fourth, fifth, and sixth centuries plainly unfold to us the rise and progress of the later style. The difference between them is specially to be noticed in the beginning of the epitaphs. A little before the middle of the fourth century we not unfrequently meet with those foolish phrases which, as time went on, became more and more in vogue, predicating of the deceased wonderful goodness and holiness, wonderful industry and prudence, wonderful innocence and wisdom, &c. Towards the end of that century and the beginning of the fifth there creep in those prosaic phrases, "Here lies," "Here rests," "Here is buried," which, after the middle of the fifth century and in the beginning of the sixth, were almost universal.

Another point of difference.
"This statement of facts, brief and incomplete as it is, will suffice to show what clear and certain marks there are whereby

Chronology of the Inscriptions. 45

we may judge concerning any undated inscription, whether it ought to be referred to the age before Constantine or after him; and if the subject were pursued further into more minute details as to the use of particular signs, words, and phrases, the certainty of our conclusions would be made even more manifest and perfectly demonstrated. Only one such particular shall be mentioned here, but it is one of universal application —to wit, the use of names; for every epitaph, however short, records at least as much as this; and this is often sufficient to tell us something about the age to which it belongs.

Number

"There is not a single dated Christian inscription after the third century in which all the three names are recorded in the ancient Roman fashion, and even the mention of two names becomes more and more rare after that date.[1] On the other hand, among the twenty-three dated inscriptions of the earlier period in which the names have been preserved, we have one instance of three names, and no less than fourteen of two.

"Then, again, there is a difference even in the names themselves. In the course of the fourth century, the names of the old Roman *gentes* gradually died away, and are hardly to be found at all on Christian epitaphs of a later date. The *cognomina* also are different; new *cognomina* are found, with a marked predilection for adjectival terminations in *entius, antius, ontius,* and *osus,* as Vincentius, Amantius, Leontius, Bonosus. Not a few also are gradually admitted which are manifestly derived from the doctrines or history of the Christian faith, or from some of its words and *formulæ;* such as Deusdedit, Adeodatus, Quodvult Deus, Anastasius, Paschasius, Martyrius, Peter, John, Thomas, Renatus, Redemptus, Refrigerius, &c.; others also perhaps from the humility of Christians and the low esteem in which they held themselves, as Stercorius, Projectus, Contumeliosus."

and character of names.

It is not, of course, meant to affirm that a hard and fast line

---

[1] An exception must be made for the name Flavius, which in the fifth and sixth centuries was in very common use as a kind of *prænomen,* and was written FL.

Occasional exceptions.

can be drawn in this matter, on neither side of which will ever be found names which we have attributed to the other side, but only that this distinction of names is most certainly, on the whole, a characteristic of different periods, so that in any large collection of epitaphs it is possible by means of it to make a very prudent conjecture as to the age to which they should be referred. And so also about the various acclamations of which we spoke first; it is not meant that they were utterly and immediately abandoned as soon as the famous Edict of Milan was published, but only that they were gradually superseded by phrases of another kind, suggested by the altered circumstances of the time; and, in like manner, it might happen that the language of a later period was, as it were, anticipated and used before its time in individual instances and under peculiar circumstances.

Inscriptions also that are written in verse, or quasi-verse, are likely to present many exceptions to the general rules of prose epitaphs of the same period. Epitaphs of this kind were never common in the Catacombs; there was no space for them on the gravestones, even if there had been a disposition to write them; and they are especially rare in the earliest ages. There is one example, however, written between the years 296 and 303, which is on every account sufficiently remarkable to be transcribed. The original may still be seen in its place in the Cemetery of St. Callixtus.[1] It runs thus:—

"The Deacon Severus made this double *cubiculum*, with its *arcisolia* and *luminare*, by order [or permission] of his Pope, Marcellinus, as a quiet abode in peace for himself and his family, to the end that it may preserve their sweet limbs in sleep through a long period of time for their Maker and Judge. Severa, sweet both to her parents and to her servants, a virgin, gave up [her life] on the 25th of January, whom the Lord with wonderful wisdom and skill[2] had ordered to be born

---

[1] See plate IX. in the new edition of our "Roma Sotterranea."
[2] This line in the original stands thus:—
QUAM DOMINUS NASCI MIRA SAPIENTIA ET ARTE JUSSERAT.
It is evidently borrowed from the *Carmen adversus Marcionæm*, usually printed with the works of Tertullian, where we read (lib. i. v. 228):—
"Quam Dominus mira sapientia fecit et arte."

in the flesh, whose body is buried here at rest in peace, until it shall rise again by means of Him who took away her soul [rendered] chaste, modest, and ever inviolate by His Holy Spirit, and which the Lord will give back again with spiritual glory. She lived nine years and eleven months and fifteen days besides. Thus was she translated from the world."

We will add yet one more general remark, for which we are indebted to De Rossi, and which the student of Christian epigraphy will often find of service in enabling him to appreciate aright some of the specimens which come before him.

He says that Christian inscriptions of most distant and dis- similar parts of the world are clearly marked by a character of wonderful unity, combined with no less striking variety; whilst there is a substantial uniformity and absolute agreement in their general tone and sense and character, yet there is, at the same time, a certain preference given to one form before another in certain localities. There are various families, so to speak, of epigraphic monuments, and each formula has its geographical as well as its chronological limits, so that it is often possible to define with tolerable certainty both the age and country to which a particular epitaph belongs by the mere study of its words and style; *e.g.*, the laudatory phrase *Bonæ memoriæ* seems to have been unknown in Rome when it was in continual use in certain parts of the provinces; *e.g.*, in Gaul. An expression of resignation to the will of God, or at least an assertion of His providence, in the statement that the deceased had ended (or would end) his term of days when God willed it (or should will it), is found in a score of epitaphs from the ancient Cemetery of Ostia, whereas it is wholly absent from those in the Cemetery of Porto on the other side of the river. The same may be said of the word *dormit*, which is rarely used in Porto, and as rarely omitted in Ostia; whilst just the reverse of this is true of the phrase *Vivas in Deo, Domino* or

Geographical as well as chronological differences.

Examples.
L.B., ii. 153.

Bull.,1866, p. 41.
1869, p. 48.

Christo. This phrase is sometimes exchanged in Porto for another, EN Kῶ XAIPEIN, bidding the dead rejoice in the Lord, *i.e.*, auguring for them full and perfect happiness in eternal life, in a form of which I do not know any examples elsewhere. In like manner, if the Christians of Capua always used the language of faith and wrote of their dead *Hic requiescit in somno pacis*, those of Beneventum were content with a terminology less distinctively Christian, and wrote *Hic situs est.*

I.R.N., i. pp. 65, 130.

Importance of observing these differences.

It would seem, then, that just as each country is apt to give some slight peculiarity to the style of architecture which it adopts, and which is common to many other countries, as each mint has its own style in reproducing even the same coins, so the Churches of different periods or different localities set their own stamp on the general forms of Christian epigraphy; and an attentive observation of these will often throw light on the history of Christian doctrine in different places, or enable us to restore an epigraph to its proper home, or to make trustworthy supplements to imperfect texts.

In pace.

It is observed by De Rossi, for example, that the phrase *In pace*, occurring so many thousands of times on Roman epitaphs, is yet hardly ever found on any of them in connection with the word *vixit*, whereas in Lyons it is found in this connection on eight stones out of the twenty which have come down to us, and very frequently indeed on Christian epitaphs in Africa. Now the Church in both those countries was much troubled by the Arian and other heresies, whence we easily comprehend why the survivors should have been anxious to declare about their deceased relatives that he or she had kept the faith, had enjoyed that *pax* of which St. Cyprian and other Fathers speak so much—the *pax ecclesiæ*, or communion with the Catholic Church. But in Rome there was not the same necessity for such a record; the words *in pace* were applied rather to the state of the soul after death than to the past condition of the living; and perhaps the very few Roman epitaphs (only eleven) in which the words are connected with life were the

Chronology of the Inscriptions. 49

epitaphs of foreigners using the fashion of their own country. On actual examination, it appears that two out of the eleven are distinctly set down as strangers (one is a Spaniard, the other *peregrinus*); the name Freda is sufficient to convict a third; in a fourth, Latin words are written in Greek letters;[1] and in two or three more the false spelling gives indications of familiarity with a foreign rather than a native pronunciation.

In like manner, M. le Blant has called attention to the remarkable fact that among all the ancient Christian inscriptions of France only those of a particular province make special mention of "the hope of the future resurrection;" and justly arguing that this cannot be the result of accident or of the mere caprice of individuals, he recognises in it a special protest against one of the heresies of the Gnostics, introduced into the country contemporaneously with Christianity itself, and laboriously refuted by St. Irenæus. An outspoken confession of faith in the resurrection of the body is fitly engraved on the tombstones of Vienne and other places in the Valley of the Rhone by the descendants of those who had had St. Irenæus for their Bishop, and who had written to their Eastern brethren so beautiful an account of the passion of their martyrs, and of the efforts made by their Pagan persecutors to destroy all trace of their remains, "to the end that they might triumph over Christ Himself, rendering impossible the regeneration of the bodies, and destroying all hope, as they said, of the resurrection."[2]

ii. p. 168 *et seq.*
" In hope of the future resurrection."

The same writer, in illustration of the advantages to be gained from the habit of noting all local peculiarities of inscriptions, very pertinently asks what sense we could have made out of such a fragment as this—

ii. p. 158.

ATTI
ΔΙΚΑ

ATTI ΔΙΚΑ.

except we had known that in the Holy Land (where it was found) it was a common practice to inscribe over the gates of towns, "This is the gate of the Lord; the just shall enter into it."

---

[1] It is printed in page 20.   [2] Euseb., H. E., v. 1.

Epitaphs of the Catacombs.

ΑΥΤΗ Η ΠΥΛΗ ΤΟΥ ΚΥΡΙΟΥ
ΔΙΚΑΙΟΙ ΕΙΣΕΛΕΥΣΟΝΤΑΙ ΕΝ ΑΥΤΗ

We will conclude this chapter with an account of the restoration of another epitaph by De Rossi, which, though it was not suggested by his familiarity with the peculiar phraseology of the period, yet certainly received much confirmation from that knowledge. The history will impress upon our readers a more lively conviction of the patient labour, the critical ingenuity, and the scrupulous conscientiousness of the discoverer than could have been derived from any mere summary of results. And as De Rossi is to be our guide throughout the following pages, it is of consequence that we should establish on as firm a basis as possible his claims to our confidence.

Epitaph of Pope Caius not found in Papal crypt. When writing in an early part of the second volume of his "Roma Sotterranea" on the Papal crypt and the place of burial of each individual Pope in the third century, he came in due course to Caius (A.D. 283-296), but he was obliged to confess that he could say little or nothing of his sepulchre; that the Liber Pontificalis says of him that he was buried on the 22d of April *in cœmeterio Callixti*—a phrase which experience had taught him was used specially to designate the Papal crypt in that cemetery; that the oldest calendars, as well as the *Martyrologium Hieronymianum* and its followers, assign the same date; but that some other martyrologies have *X. Kal. Maias,* instead of *X. Kal. Martias,* or rather they have both dates; that different explanations had been given of this, but for his own part he thought it evident that some copyist had first made the very easy blunder of writing *Martias* for *Maias,* and then another had inserted both; but he added that it was far more difficult to account for yet a third commemoration assigned to him in some martyrologies on the 1st of July; he would only say that he was not himself satisfied with the explanation suggested by the learned editor of the *Martyrologium Hieronymianum,* the Bollandists, and others, who had recourse to the theory of some translations of the saint's body at various times, of which no record had reached us.

Chronology of the Inscriptions. 51

This was the state of his knowledge on the subject in 1868. In 1875 or 1876, when writing the early part of the third volume he interrupts his narrative to tell us of certain fragments, which he has found near the crypt of St. Eusebius, of a slab of very fine Greek marble, beautifully engraved, with Greek letters of unusual size, and cut more deeply than usual, and the words separated from one another by a very peculiar ornamental figure, which he had seen before on a Christian epitaph of the year 291, and published in his volume on the Christian inscriptions.

Fragments of it discovered elsewhere.

I.C., i. p. 24.

"Having hunted," he says, "with great diligence for every fragment of this slab, however small, and studied attentively how the broken bits should be put together (for unfortunately many of them did not fit into one another), at last I saw, and after much deliberation I was convinced, that they belong to the sepulchre of Pope Caius. When I wrote the second volume, and treated of the Papal crypt, I had not succeeded in putting the fragments together, so I could not make any use of them, though the inscription really illustrates the matter which belongs to that volume. The study of minute fragments, the distinguishing amid so enormous and confused a mass the bits that belong to the same inscription, is an undertaking so long and wearisome, and is often interfered with by so many even material hindrances, that if a conscientious determination to fulfil what has been enjoined me and what I have promised to do in this work did not oblige me, and if the ordinarily moderate fruit which I reap from so much labour were not occasionally multiplied a hundredfold by some unlooked-for discovery, my patience would have failed, and I should not have persevered. Let so much be said by way of apology and explanation why I bring forth to the world to-day so remarkable a monument, when its proper place should have been in the preceding volume; and now, without further preface, let us come to the point."

R.S., iii. 115.

He then gives all the fragments of the slab on which there

52   *Epitaphs of the Catacombs.*

The whole restored.
are any letters or parts of letters, or any of the ornamental stops we have spoken of. They are the darkly shaded portions of the following diagram :—

Restoration justified.
The reader will observe that the relative positions of the ΕΠ in the first line, the Τ in the second, and the ΜΑΙ in the third are fixed with certainty by the way in which the three fragments of stone dovetail into one another, and it was the arrangement of these three bits which ultimately gave the key to the whole. In like manner, the relative positions of the Υ in the first line, ΚΑ in the second, and Λ in the third, were determined with the same absolute certainty. It remained only to assign their proper places to ΠΡ and to Γ; but even of these it was certain that ΠΡ belonged to the last line, because of the long uninscribed portion of marble below them; and of Γ, that it was the initial letter of a word, because of the point before it. Having thus arranged his fragments, De Rossi proceeds as follows :—

"The arrangement, now that it has been made, is so evidently correct that it will seem strange that I should have been delayed so long and laboured so hard to make it. The epitaph begins with the proper name of the deceased in the genitive case; then follows ΕΠ, which in so noble a monument naturally suggests that he was a Bishop; and then in

Chronology of the Inscriptions. 53

the two lower lines the burial (καταθεσις, *depositio*) is assigned to some day in the latter half of April; and the deceased man's name began with Γ. Now, of all the Popes and Bishops buried in the Cemetery of Callixtus whose names have been preserved to us by ancient documents, the only one whose name begins with Γ is Caius, who was buried on the 22d of April 296; and it has been already mentioned that the singular stops between the words have been found precisely on an epitaph of about that time (291). Moreover, the abbreviation KAT is found on a whole group of epitaphs belonging to this very place and period. Thus everything conspires to confirm the reading we have suggested, and the supplements we have made to these mutilated fragments of a noble epitaph. A most attentive analysis of the epitaph, and of the beautifully symmetrical form of the letters convinces me that this is not a mere happy play of fancy, not a mere specious probability, but a true and solid reality. It is scarcely credible that it should be an entirely fortuitous and deceitful combination of circumstances, in such wonderful harmony with one another, which recalls to us the memory of Pope Caius."

He then shows, by a still more minute analysis of the arrangement of the letters and stops, that there could only have been two or three letters after ΕΠ, and that the name at the beginning can only have consisted of five or six letters; and so, he says, "the intrinsic and historical reasons which justify his restoration are still further confirmed by extrinsic reasons and material facts." Finally, on the ninth fragment of the stone, which has not yet been mentioned, is found a *graffito* of the name of *Leo*, preceded by a cross, the same as appears on the sepulchre of Cornelius and elsewhere, and which clearly shows that this was no common tomb. In addition to all these arguments, "the very drawing of the epitaph as restored will satisfy, if I am not mistaken, every practised eye and every competent judge that it is no result of ingenious combination, but a happy discovery of the truth."

Another epitaph restored.

P. 260.

Thus wrote De Rossi at p. 115 of the third volume of his Roma Sotterranea. A hundred and fifty pages farther on, when all that preceded had been (he tells us) already printed, he has something more to say on the same subject, and it is too intimately connected with the whole argument of this volume for us not to make room for his narrative. He had found in another part of the cemetery sixteen fragments of another large slab, which had evidently served as the *mensa* of an *arcosolium*, and from which he was able to gather that a certain Jovina had bought an *arcosolium* in the Cemetery of Callixtus, near the tomb of some martyr (*Arcosolium in Callisti at Domn...*). This discovery was of great interest and value even in its imperfect state; not only because it speaks of St. Callixtus' (omitting the word cemetery) exactly as it is written in the old calendars which were published by F. Dionysius Filocalus in 354, just when this part of the cemetery was in use, but also because it confirmed with a seal of absolute certainty what De Rossi had already announced as the result of his own personal examination: that this Liberian district (so to call this part of the Catacomb, from the Pope in whose time it was made) had no specific name of its own, but was considered a part of the famous cemetery with which it was connected. But the inscription would have been a hundredfold more interesting and more valuable if it had not been broken off precisely at the middle of the word *Domn*. This was the second time he had been thus cruelly disappointed by the mutilated condition of an inscription which seemed to promise important revelations, and the most diligent search was therefore made for the missing fragments. The search was unsuccessful; so, having resigned himself as best he might, he set to work to make the most of what he had, and read a paper upon it to an academic audience. He has given us some account of this paper, rightly judging that, in the light of later discoveries, it would be both amusing and instructive; teaching, he says, a lesson as to the caution that is necessary in pronouncing judgment in cases of

Chronology of the Inscriptions. 55

this kind, and at the same time leading to a most unexpected discovery of the truth.

The first line of the inscription began, as he then supposed, with *merenti Jovinæ ;* and he considered it to be quite perfect on that side, *i.e.*, on the left-hand side as one looks at the stone, so that all his energies were concentrated on an attempt to supply what was wanting on the right-hand side, or at the end of each line. First, he determined that not more than five or six letters could be supplied in any line; and this he judged, first from what he saw of the last two lines, which needed no supplement at all; and secondly, from the supplements which were obviously required in the first three lines to complete the words coj*ugem*, de*cessit*, and comp*aravit*. Unless then the fourth line were prolonged out of all proportion to the others, there was only room here also for very few letters. This being assumed, it would seem to follow that the *ita* at the beginning of the fifth line could not be the ending of the word *deposita* (as would otherwise have been thought certain), but must form part of the missing name of the saint; wherefore he suggested *at Domna*(*m*) *Soterita*(*m*), the name of the martyr St. Soteris being sometimes found declined in this corrupt form instead of *Soteridem*, and the final *m* being often suppressed in writing in the Catacombs, as it evidently was in familiar conversation. Another adjacent area of this cemetery bears the name of this very martyr, and an example could be found to prove that *ad martyrem* did not always mean an immediate and material contiguity of the two sepulchres, but only a certain general and moral proximity; *e.g.*, a husband and wife were buried in the portico of the Vatican Basilica, yet they described their tomb as *ad Sanctum Petrum Apostolum*, though it was a long way off from the "confession" where the body of the Apostle lay. Finally, he observed as a singular coincidence that the *Natale* of St. Soteris was the very day on which the lady whose epitaph was under consideration is stated to have been buried. What conclusion then could seem more obvious and certain than that he had hit upon the correct restitution of the missing letters?

De Rossi himself, however, was not well satisfied with his own explanation. All the instances of *ad martyrem* hitherto found in the Catacombs had seemed to denote material contiguity; the example of its use in a wider sense belonged to a later period. Moreover, the inscription seemed imperatively to require *deposita*; it would have been very strange indeed if that word had been omitted, and so the inscription had announced that Jovina had bought the tomb on such a day, but made no mention of the day on which she had occupied it. A learned colleague also called attention to the strange way in which the inscription must have been arranged, the letters touching the very edge of the stone on the left-hand side, whilst yet there must have been a quantity of unoccupied space on the right. Was it possible that the stone had been cut in half, and that they had only half the inscription before them? This led to a more minute inspection of the monument itself; and it was discovered that, in the upper corner of the left-hand side, a bit of mortar, which it had never occurred to them to rub off, covered the letter E. *Merenti* had been a possible word; *emerenti* was impossible. It must certainly have been *benemerenti*, and there must be another section of the stone somewhere. And then it flashed upon De Rossi's memory that he had found a few months before, at some distance from this part of the cemetery, yet in the same quarter, a section of an inscription, containing many letters, which gave no sense whatever. The reader may be sure that no time was lost in bringing the two fragments together, and our diagram on the next page shows the result.

Strange to say, the fragments originally discovered had given the endings of nearly all the lines, so that there was hardly any need of supplements where it had been attempted to make them; the supplements were wanted at the beginning of the lines, where all had been supposed to be perfect; and in most instances they were precisely what had been suggested. Only the beginning of the last line was new, and made a most unexpected revelation, that the saint whose name had been so eagerly sought for was not St. Soteris, but Caius. The reader will say that the name does not follow the title *Domnum* immediately, a whole line intervenes. But he will also see that, as the inscription was first engraved, the two words did follow each other without any interruption whatever; at first there were only five lines, written at regular intervals; the line which records the date of the burial is a manifest addition, squeezed in between lines four and five, to the complete destruction of the symmetry of the engraving.

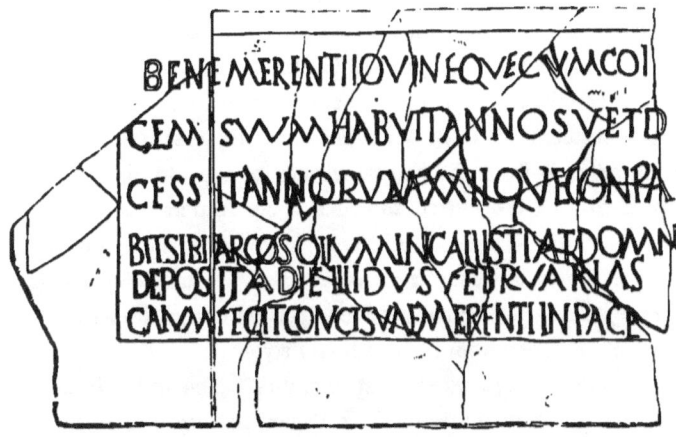

BENEMERENTI JOVINE QUE CUM COJ*u*
GEM SUUM HABUIT ANNOS V ET D*e*
CESSIT ANNORUM XXII QUE CONPA*ra*
BIT SIBI ARCOSOLIUM IN CALLISTI AT DOMN*um*
DEPOSITA DIE III IDUS FEBRUARIAS
GAIUM FECIT COJUGI SUÆ MERENTI IN PACE

"To the well-deserving Jovina, who spent five years with her husband, and died at the age of twenty-two years; who bought for herself an arcosolium in St. Callixtus' near St. Gaius. [Her husband] put this up to his deserving wife. In peace. She was buried on the 11th of February."

CHAPTER IV.

PAGAN EPITAPHS.

Necessity of studying Pagan epitaphs—Points of contrast—To Pagans, death was without hope; an eternal farewell—Yet imaginary exchange of salutations between the living and the dead—Sepulchres—Sententiæ sepulchrales on the vanity of life expressed under a variety of images—Different views taken of life; sensual, practical, trifling, enigmatical, serious—Testimony given by the epitaphs to the state of domestic life in Rome—Strong expressions of natural affection—Parents and children—Impatience at untimely death—Husbands and wives—Some titles of praise or affection perhaps only conventional—Yet the facts recorded are true and very creditable—Domestic virtues praised in women.

Necessity of studying Pagan epitaphs.

ANOTHER essential requisite in a student of ancient Christian epigraphy is a competent knowledge of the Pagan epigraphy of the same period. Without this knowledge he will certainly fail to recognise many Christian epitaphs when he sees them, and he will probably claim as fruits of Christian teaching certain excellencies of character which can be shown to have resulted also—in some instances at least, and to a certain degree—from the natural virtues of the old Romans. Thus, it may have occurred to some of our readers that there is not much evidence of Christianity in most of the epitaphs recorded in our last chapter; and yet a slight familiarity with Pagan epitaphs would have at once suggested several important points of difference from their ordinary style.

Points of contrast.

De Rossi has remarked, that the most ancient Christian epitaphs differ from those of their Pagan contemporaries, not so much in what they say as in what they do not say. They omit, for example, the customary dedication to the *Dî Manes*. They say nothing about having made provision for the burial

Pagan Epitaphs. 59

of other members of the family, because in most instances each grave can only hold one body, or at most two or three; they are silent as to the birth and parentage, the country, the profession and social rank of the deceased; and after the middle of the third century, they rarely record more than one of his names. At first, also, they hardly ever make mention of the relationship between the deceased and the person setting up the *titulus*, a particular which is seldom omitted by the surviving friends or relatives of a deceased Pagan. They contain no appeal to the good feeling or religious superstition of passers-by not to violate or in any way profane the tomb, nor do they utter imprecations against those who do. These marks of difference may be observed even in the briefest inscriptions; in those which are longer, the contrast between the two classes would naturally be still more visible. In order that we may be able to judge of this, we will first pass in review the leading features of Pagan epitaphs, as they may be gathered from the thousands of examples which have come down to us and been preserved in various collections; and then in the following chapters we will do the same for the Christian epitaphs.

The first point which strikes us in studying any collection of Pagan epitaphs is the dreary prospect, or rather the utter want of prospect, of anything beyond the grave, which seems to be their chief characteristic. Occasionally an attempt is made to conceal this by apostrophising the shades below and begging them to welcome the deceased, as though into another world; *e.g.*, *To the Pagans death was without hope of future life.*

> OSSA NICENIS HIC SITA SUNT.
> SUPERI, VIVITE, VALETE;
> INFERI, HAVETE, RECIPITE NICENEM.[1]
>
> The bones of Nicen are buried here.
> Ye who live in the upper air, live on, farewell;
> Ye shades below, hail; receive Nicen.

Or again, a husband addresses his deceased wife, bids her rest well, and asks her, if the shades below have any sense (*si quid*

[1] Pitture e sepolcri scoperti sull' Esquilino nell' 1875. Par Edoardo Brizio, No. 473.

sapiunt), to remember him; "we shall never forget thee."[1]
More commonly, however, death is described as a never-ending
sleep, and the grave as the last everlasting home; and the
deceased, contemplating himself and all that he is and has,
says that he leaves behind him an empty name; that his body
is dissolved into dust, and his life into the air. Again, the
same idea was conveyed in the quiet sadness of that one word
Vale, or in the more impassioned repetition of it, *Vale, vale,
dulcissima; semper in perpetuo vale*—the last long eternal farewell, which is frequently all that is added to the name, age,
and relationship of the deceased. In some places, *e.g.*, in
Majorca, the favourite formula for expressing this melancholy
truth consisted of two words only, *Fuisti; vale*, which may be
considered very fairly to express the popular belief upon the
subject, whatever faint hopes of a brighter kind may have
dawned upon the minds of a few select philosophers.

This mode of taking leave of the dead, indicating the nature
of the separation which had now befallen them, and the insuperable barrier which henceforth intervened between them and
the living, had at least the merit of being simple and natural.
We cannot say the same of another formula, which was frequently united with it, and which imagined an interchange of
salutations between the person buried and those who passed by
his tomb. These were invited to salute the deceased with an
ave or *salve*, and the imaginary response stood engraven on
the stone ready for all comers. It is even expressly recorded
upon some monuments that this was the reason why they were
placed near the highways, that the deceased might receive these
mock salutations more frequently, *T. Lollius positus propter
viam, ut dicant prætereuntes, Lolli, Ave.*

A third form of salutation which is often given and asked
for in the inscriptions is of a somewhat different kind—not
unnatural, but inane; we mean the prayer (so to call it) of

---

[1] Pitture e sepolcri scoperti sull' Esquilino nell' 1875. Par Edoardo Brizio, No. 182.

Pagan Epitaphs.

the survivors that the bones of the deceased may rest well, or (much more commonly) that the earth may lie lightly upon him. This same conceit is to be found in some of the Greek epitaphs collected in the "Anthologia Græca," of one of which Merivale has given the following pleasing translation :—

> "Hail, Universal Mother! lightly rest
> On that dead form,
> Which, when with life invested, ne'er oppressed
> Its fellow-worm."

By the Romans it was not so poetically expressed, but it was in more general use. In their burial-places, both at home and abroad, it was so common, that the initials of the words constituting the formula were used almost as frequently as the words themselves. S.T.T.L. may be seen nearly as often at the end of a Pagan epitaph in ancient Rome as R.I.P. at the end of a Christian one in the modern city. And as the words *Sit tibi terra levis* form half of a pentameter line, other words were often added to make the other half, such as *Dicite qui legitis, Dic rogo qui transis, Te rogo præteriens, Omnes optamus, Ossibus opto tuis*, or the like; and then these phrases, too, were so frequently repeated, that they in their turn were abridged into mere initials. Promises were held out to induce passers-by to stop and repeat these words—promises of a long life or of a happy death; they are implored not to grudge the few moments which the repetition would require, or are reminded that the deceased deserved such an attention, because he (or she) was never burdensome to any during life. When the stereotyped form of words was departed from, the result was occasionally grotesque, as when an appeal is made to the gravestone not to press heavily, out of consideration for the tender age of the child that lies beneath it. Sometimes it was travestied, as in a malicious epigram of Martial, the original of which may be found in the Greek Anthology,[1] praying that the earth covering the deceased may be light and soft as sand,

Sometimes travestied.

---

[1] Martial, ix. 30; Anthol. Græc., xi. 226.

that so the dogs may more readily get at the bones. Outrages of this kind, however, are very rare; for, to the credit of Pagan epitaphs, it must be stated that they are for the most part remarkably free from those exhibitions of ill-nature, misplaced facetiousness, or other forms of bad taste, which are but too commonly found in any collection of epitaphs of our own country.

To these ordinary *formulæ*, which may be said to have been common to all Pagan epitaphs in Rome, it was not unusual to add some appropriate sentiment in prose or verse, more commonly the latter. These vary considerably in character, but most of them will fall under one or other of the following heads. First, we find, as might have been expected, in Pagan as well as Christian epitaphs, certain commonplaces about the shortness and uncertainty of life, the inevitable fate of death, the deceitfulness of fortune, the vanity of care, the bitter disappointment of broken hopes, and the unprofitableness of grief. These sentiments are often expressed in forms which, like some English epitaphs, became public property, and were repeated in every graveyard, so to speak. Here is one of the most common:—*Decipimur votis, et tempore fallimur; et mors Deridet curas; anxia vita nihil.* Sometimes they are expressed under images with which all ages seem to have been familiar. Thus life is compared to a journey, or again to a stage on which each man plays his part. "Hallo, here, you weary traveller; however far you may walk, you must come here at last." A father burying his daughter expresses his thoughts by a very homely simile: "Men fall like apples," he says, "some when they are young and sour, others when they are mellow and ripe."

Some profess to make a mock at death, and bid men live and enjoy themselves whilst they live; live like a gentleman (*quomodo condecet ingenuum*); live for the present hour, drink and play, because they are sure of nothing, and only what they eat and drink is really theirs. "Live joyfully whilst you live.

Pagan Epitaphs. 63

Life is a trifling gift. Presently it begins, grows strong by degrees, and then by degrees fades away." "Fortune makes many promises, but keeps none of them. Live, then, for the present day and hour, since nothing else is really ours." Some recommend a diligent practical worship of Venus and Bacchus, in the coarsest terms; others only record their past potations and other sensual indulgences; and whilst allowing that these things have been the ruin of their bodies, console themselves with the reflection that after all these are what make up life. Some speak of the change from life to death in a very quiet matter-of-fact way: "I have lived and struggled for eighty years that I might come to this home at last, full of joy; now I shall be quiet, and stay here always." "I have been seeking gain all my life, and always losing. Now death has come, and I can't do either the one or the other. I hope you who read this will live happy." "Here I am where I never was before." "Take heart, no one lives for ever; even Hercules died at last." One man exclaims in a careless jaunty way, "I lived as I like, but I don't know why I died." Another, "You who read this, go and bathe in the temple of Apollo hard by, as I have done before now with my wife. I would do it now, if I could." Another, in a more dogged, sullen tone, "Here it is; so it is; nothing else could be." Another speaks as if he were perplexed: "Once I was not; now I am not; I know nothing about it; it does not concern me." A fourth and a fifth would fain perplex others: "I was not, and I am, and I shall not be. It causes me no pain;" and "Here I am, and I am not;" which last may bring to our recollection those more elaborate Christian enigmas which are sometimes to be met with in English churchyards, both in Latin and English forms, *e.g.*, in the churchyard of Amwell, near Ware, Hertfordshire:

> "That which a being was, what is it? show;
> That being which it was, it is not now.
> To be what 'tis, is *not* to be, you see;
> That which now is not, shall a being be."

[margin: 6234. 7411. 4816. Practical. 4818. 7402. 4805. Trifling. 4812. 4803. G., 819, 4. Enigmatical. O.H., 4810, 4811.]

Serious.	Occasionally we meet with a man who took a more serious view of life, and made some kind of review of his own past history, but, as might have been expected, more after the
7412.	fashion of the Pharisee than of the publican; *e.g.*, "I have restored everything committed to my trust; I have not committed adultery; I have not been quarrelsome; I have done what I could." Or again, "I have been pious and holy; I lived as long as I could; I have never had any lawsuit or quarrel, or grumbling or debts; I have been always faithful to my friends;
C. I.L., vi. 2489.	I had a small fortune but a great mind." "I have always lived as a poor man, but well and honourably, never defrauding any; which [I hope] may benefit my bones."

It is indeed a melancholy task to review the old Pagan epitaphs, either with reference to the testimony they give as to the popular belief on the condition of the dead, or the insight they afford into the feelings and aspirations of the individual human soul. Let us now look at them in another and far more pleasing aspect, viz., the evidence they offer as to the state of domestic life among the Romans. And here we are

Natural affection strongly expressed.

struck with the tokens of strong natural affection between parents and children, husbands and wives, which meet us at every turn. Even these are too frequently tainted by an ill-concealed or an avowed rebellion of the heart and will against the dispensations of Providence, which has inverted the natural order of succession by calling away the children before the parents, or destroyed a happy home which had been enjoyed but for too brief a time. We will speak of each class of epitaphs in its turn; and first of those which were set up to the memory of children.

Parents and children.

O.H., 4793.

We have already alluded to the want of resignation which is one of their special characteristics; *e.g.*, a young lady is made to speak in her own proper person (not by the mouth of her parents), and she speaks thus: "I lift up my hands"—and the hands stand there carved between the letters, suiting the action to the word—"I lift up my hands against God who took me

Pagan Epitaphs. 65

away, though I had done no harm, at the age of twenty."
And a boy invites all who read the memorial of his sad fate,
cut off in his tenth year, to "curse the harshness of his lot." *O.H.*, 4579.
One parent merely says that "the fates judged ill" when they
robbed him of his child. Another, who laments the loss of
five relatives in one day—a wife and child, a brother, sister,
and nephew; the nature of the accident is not told—records
his loss by saying that "the angry gods gave all five in one   4796.
day to everlasting sleep." The bereaved parents commonly
inscribe themselves *miserrimi, infelicissimi;* or sometimes they
apply these epithets to the children who have died. Mothers 4583, 4591, 4602.
especially burst forth into passionate lamentations over their
blighted hopes, describing themselves as "left to tears and
groans," "condemned to perpetual darkness and daily miserable lamentation." Sometimes they speak more moderately,
and only complain of the unnatural cruelty of fate which has
obliged them to perform the last sad offices of burial for their
children, which the children ought rather to have performed
for them. One father, who seems to have lost his daughter by
some accident or violence, desires that he may be buried with
her, that so his bones may be mixed with hers, which will be
some consolation to him. He also desires that there may be
buried with him all the tokens of mourning which he had pre-
pared during life—a couch with coverlets, and a cloak, all
black. To the freedman, through whose fault he had lost her,
he leaves a nail and a rope, that he may hang himself.

Once only do we find the sentiment expressed by Pagan
parents which is not unfrequent on the lips of Christians, that
an early death is a token of God's love. They had lost a child
of three years old, and they write, "*Quam Di amaverunt, hæc
moritur infa(n)s.*" In another instance, it is said of a boy who
died when he was nine, that he had asked that he might die
before his parents. But far more commonly, whether the
epitaph be put into the mouth of the child or of the parents,
the sentiment expressed is one of disappointment and disgust at

E

the premature loss of life and enjoyment, and extinction of bright hopes. Thus a young lady of twelve, who had begun to entertain thoughts of matrimony (or her friends for her), "laments the end of her fate." A child complains that "it has not been allowed him to live beyond seven months," "defrauded of my eighth year," "cut off by an untimely death," &c. And parents utter similar complaints for their children. "Alas! to how bitter a fate have you been abandoned. Before your term of life was ended, you were given over to death, and you died when you ought to be flourishing in your youth." "Orcus has taken from me him in whom was my hope." "Our hope was in our boy; now all is ashes and lamentations;" and they are constantly said to have died "without having deserved it." One bereaved mother begs her son to receive her without delay to himself; another having lost her son, "hated life," and dies, either of a broken heart or possibly by suicide, a fortnight later; and a third utters a word of warning, that wives should not desire to become mothers, because of the pain of parting with their children.

The regretful memories of bereaved parents sometimes led them to record on their children's gravestones not only their moral excellences, which might very suitably be commemorated there, but their intellectual, and even their physical gifts of talent, learning, grace, beauty, and the rest. Thus a boy of sixteen is represented as saying of himself that he had always loved his studies, been reverential to his masters, obeyed the commands of his parents; another boy of fifteen is styled *puer reverentissimus*. To a little girl of seven a very pleasing epitaph is inscribed: that she was obedient to her mother, and a favourite with everybody—*matri obsequens, placita omnibus*. Of others, the innocence and simplicity are commended; and these, of course, are generally the very young. On a Roman sarcophagus, found at York, we read *Animæ innocentissimæ* for a child who had only lived ten months; and the same, in Spain, for children of eight or eleven years. All this is natural

Pagan Epitaphs. 67

and pleasing enough, but we are struck by a certain sense of incongruity when we find on the memorials of the youthful dead a panegyric of talent which has never been developed, or of beauty which is now corruption, such as we find recorded of a youthful bride, not yet sixteen, that she was "of exquisite form and marvellous beauty," and "that her mind was truly worthy of her body;" of a girl of nine, that she was "of singular beauty, most affectionate manners, and learning most excellent, beyond what might lawfully have been expected in one of her age and sex;" of another, of eleven, that just when she had become most learned—her mistress having taught her all arts—she was cruelly taken away; and of several, both boys and girls, that "their talents surpassed their age." One boy of sixteen is said to have "surpassed even old men in wisdom, and never to have had anything in common with youth." Of a girl, her skill in music and grace in dancing are thought worthy of commemoration on her tomb; and the fond mother of another calls upon all strangers who have any feeling to pour forth sighs, and to fill with tears the hollow recess provided for this purpose in the marble urn, for that "beauty's model perished when her daughter (Lyda) died." Another bitterly laments that neither wit, nor amiability, nor loving winning ways (*blanditiæ*), had been of any avail to prolong his child's days; spite of them all, he had become "the foul prey of the brutal Pluto."[1]

We come next to the epitaphs which commemorate husbands and wives. And here we cannot help remarking that it has been most unfortunate for the posthumous fame of Roman matrons and *patres-familias* of the Imperial period, that Juvenal should have attained the supremacy he has in our schools and colleges, to the exclusion of his more amiable, and, as we think, more trustworthy contemporary, Pliny the Younger. If we are to believe Juvenal, there were hardly more honest women in Rome than there were gates to Thebes

Husbands and wives.

[1] Sepolcri scoperti sull' Esquilino nell', 1875, par E. Brizio, No. 223.

or mouths to the Nile; yet the letters of Pliny alone supply us with a number of very charming portraits among his own acquaintances. According to Juvenal, divorce was the almost normal result of Roman marriage; he tells us of one lady who had had eight husbands in five years, and of others who counted their husbands by the years of their marriageable life. But the epitaphs tell a different tale; and although this class of monuments does not enjoy the highest reputation for truthfulness, yet their testimony cannot be lightly set aside. We may call in question some of their epithets, and insist on making serious deductions from their superlatives; but we can hardly refuse credence to the facts which they record.

Some epithets perhaps only conventional.

Benemerenti, for example, is a specimen of an epithet to which we need not attach much value; hardly, perhaps, any meaning at all, since we find it given to infants who could not have earned a title to the gratitude of survivors. Then, again, we should be disposed to relegate to the same category of fashionable unmeaning compliments, the praise of amiability (*dulcis, dulcissima*) as applied to deceased husbands or wives. No doubt it was used with perfect sincerity in many instances, but it was used so uniformly that its omission would have been almost singular, and suggested invidious comparisons. We are suspicious, too, of such superlative and hyperbolical language as *incomparabilis, miræ sapientiæ*, and *probitatis, rarissimi exempli*, and the like, epithets which we shall find very fashionable on Christian monuments of the latter half of the fourth century, and which are not wanting in the Pagan collections we are now examining. We are much confirmed in our suspicion of the worthlessness of these titles by the fact that when once they had been introduced into the burial-place of any town or village, they were apt to be repeated there again and again—*e.g.*, at least, a score of times on the monuments in Beneventum, though there is no reason why such paragons of perfection should have been monopolised by certain favoured localities. For the same reason, we do not believe that the

Pagan Epitaphs.

Roman gentlemen and ladies who lived and died in Spain or Africa loved one another in any special degree above their fellow-countrymen and women in other parts of the Empire, or were remarkable in any singular manner for the possession of a very ordinary quality, which is nevertheless incessantly attributed to them on their tombstones—viz., kindness to their relatives and friends. We gather only that it had become the fashion of those particular colonies to publish this encomium on the dead; and the fashion was so universally followed that the initials *c.* (or *k.*), *s.*, and *p.*, *i.*, and *s.*, are often made to do duty for the whole phrase—*carus suis, pius in suos*. *C.I.L.*, ii. 1733, 2257, &c., 1138, 1420, &c.

After making all these deductions, however, and others perhaps which need not be enumerated, there still remains a sufficient body of testimony to be gathered from these epitaphs which will serve to rehabilitate to a certain degree the characters of many a Roman matron and her husband. It will show that the natural virtues were by no means wanting in Pagan Rome, even when Juvenal was painting his hideous portrait of their manners, and it engenders a strong suspicion as to the general trustworthiness of the portrait. For, if divorce was so easy as we know from the law books that it was, and if it was also so common as the satirist represents, whence comes it that we have so many scores and hundreds of epitaphs, testifying that husband and wife have lived together for 15, 20, 30, 40, 50, and even 60 (in one instance, 68) years, *sine ullâ querelâ, sine ulla contumeliâ, sine læsione animi, sine ullâ offensâ, sine ullo stomacho, sine jurgio, sine ullâ bile, sine lite molestâ?* Pericles told the Athenian ladies that their highest merit would be, to be but little spoken of, either for praise or blame, by those outside their own household; and one of the Roman epitaphs before us, set up by a son to his mother, laments that it is difficult for a woman to earn new praises because of the quiet uniform character of her occupations and duties, so that the panegyric of all good ladies, he says, must needs be simple and uniform. And certainly the best womanly virtues are

Yet the facts recorded are true, and very creditable.

Domestic virtues of women praised.

recognised in detail and praised in these Pagan monuments. Modesty and chastity, prudence, skill, and diligence in the management of household affairs, the habit of staying at home, industry, gentleness, and other such qualities, are items of eulogy, applied not indiscriminately, yet not rarely, to Roman wives and mothers; and we see no reason to doubt that the widowers who gave this praise to their wives meant what they said. Once or twice we find a woman praised for never having been the wife of more than one husband. Twice a husband praises his wife, or a son his mother, because she nursed her own children. Again and again, the survivor testifies to the imperturbable good nature of her whom he has lost:—"She never gave a bad word to her husband;" "I never received from her any insult or bad word;" "I never had any complaint to make of her at all;" "She never committed any fault except by dying;" and "I never received any pain from her except by her death." There are other epitaphs also of these Pagan husbands departing from the ordinary track, and having a sufficiently definite character of their own to deserve quotation. One, for example, who had lived with his wife for thirteen years, "with great sweetness" declares that "though dead, she will always be alive to him, and always be golden in his eyes." Another says of his wife, that he loved her better than himself, and that their union was such, nothing but death could separate them. Another deceased wife is praised as "chaste, modest, irreproachable;" "a mother to all the world, one who came to the help of all who were in need, and who never saddened any one." A third widower whose married life had lasted eighteen years *sine querelâ*, swears that his regret for his loss is so keen and absorbing that he will never marry again. And a fourth makes loud lamentations, and calls upon the Manes, and entreats Pluto to restore to him his wife, who had lived with him in such harmony until the fatal day; and then, addressing herself, he begs that she will obtain from the Manes, *if there be such spirits*, that he may not any longer suffer this accursed separation; finally, he prays that the earth may lie light upon her, since she never did any injury on earth, and "if any one ever injured her, may he be rejected by the gods above and by the gods below, and may the earth lie heavy upon him."

Side by side with these should be set a few specimens of the epitaphs of widows to their deceased husbands. One begins by saying that they had been bound to one another in love ever since they were a boy and girl (*puer et puella*), that they had been married but a short time, and that even during much of that short time they had been cruelly separated by circumstances. Wherefore she makes a passionate appeal to the Manes to have her husband in good keeping, to be kind and indulgent to him, to allow her to see him in her dreams, and, finally, to enable her speedily to rejoin him. Another, in Tarracona, appeals to the Manes, if they have any sense or feeling (*si saperent*), to withdraw her also from life, since it is no longer enjoyable without her husband, who was her *light* (*dulcem carui lucem cum te amisi*); and she concludes by begging that if the abundant tears she sheds for him are of any avail, he will come and show himself to her in dreams at night. A third widow—the last whose words we will quote—having made a common sepulchre for herself and her husband, prays that "having spent a pleasant life together for twenty-five years in peace and harmony (*æquabili concordiâ*), they may not be separated even in the grave."

To these we may add the following epitaph set up by one freedman to the memory of another:—"Aulus Memmius Urbanus to Aulus Memmius Clarus, my dearest fellow-freedman.—Between me and thee, my most excellent (*sanctissime*) fellow-freedman, I know not that there has ever been any quarrel; and here on this epitaph I call the gods above and below to bear witness to my statement. We met together first in the slave-market, and in one and the same house we received our liberty; nor could anything have ever separated us but this thy fatal day."

On the whole, then, we may say that there is a very pleasing display of all the natural affections on the Pagan monuments of Ancient Rome. They are only dumb, or give utterance to painful and discordant sounds, so far as any supernatural hope is concerned. Their utterances of sorrow are often most expressive in their brevity, as where the parents of a "very dear" boy of twelve and a girl of six merely state that they "*deceperunt una unoque lecto elati*,"[1] "disappointed their hopes at the same time, and were carried out to their graves on one bier." But if they venture to look beyond the grave, all is dark and dreary. The parents of two girls who had died young may dare to inscribe a challenge on their tomb that if anybody doubts of the existence of the disembodied spirits, he should make some vow or promise (*sponsione factâ*), and then invoke them, and he will learn; a husband may boldly call his wife, or a son his parents, divine, a god, or a goddess; but, speaking generally, there was but one view of the day of death presented to the heathen mind—viz., that it was

Perfidus, infelix, horrificusque dies.

---

[1] In an inscription let into the wall of the staircase at No. 17 Piazza d'Ara Cœli, Rome, the residence of Commendatore de Rossi.

CHAPTER V.

THE TEACHING OF CHRISTIAN EPITAPHS ABOUT DEATH AND THE DEAD.

Contrast between Pagan and Christian epitaphs—Christian epigraphy perfected by degrees, but its general character shown from the first; simple, hopeful, and joyous; less religious in the fourth and later centuries—Life and love characteristics of the most ancient epitaphs—Some exceptions, chiefly of later date—An episcopal instruction on death in the third century—Language of epitaphs denotes belief in future resurrection—Acclamations for the dead; of life in God, peace, refreshment—These phrases and some others explained—The same prayers found in the Liturgies, ancient and modern—Prayers addressed to the dead by surviving friends and relatives—Religious character of these prayers and their orthodoxy.

OUT of the almost innumerable monumentat inscriptions of Pagan Rome which have reached us, we have sought in our last chapter to gather as clear an idea as we could of the notions entertained by their authors as to the existence of a future state; and we have seen that not one affirms it, though the hearts of many manifestly yearned after it. Affectionate hearts could not bear to think that they were hopelessly and eternally separated from those whom they had loved so truly when alive; and with hesitating tongue, therefore, and in images borrowed from poetry, they call upon the inexorable Manes to deal mercifully with the departed, or to take compassion upon the survivors, and to bring back the image of the beloved in dreams and visions of the night. The Christian inscriptions, on the other hand, imply, even when they do not actually express, a firm belief in the reality of a future life: they pray for the dead as though they were still living, and capable of feeling joy and sorrow; or they call upon them for assistance

Contrast between Pagan and Christian epitaphs.

74   *Epitaphs of the Catacombs.*

as though they were still able to give it; and often the very language in which they speak of death and all that concerns it bears within it an unconscious testimony to faith in a future resurrection.

We do not say that there is no exception to this rule. It ought not to be a matter of surprise to any one to hear that amid the thousands of Christian epitaphs written in the same city during the same period as that from which we derived our estimate of the Pagan view of life and death, it is possible to find an occasional specimen which approaches more nearly to the Pagan than the Christian type, though perhaps some would hardly have expected that this should have happened more frequently in the fourth and fifth than in the preceding centuries. But at any rate, everybody must see that it would be quite unreasonable to expect that there could have been created all at once, in the first moment that Christianity began, a distinctly Christian epigraphy. As in art, so in inscriptions also, the Church would at first merely drop from the general usage of the day all that was contrary to the faith, and then in due time would bring forth new fruit of her own. But as the very first efforts of Christian art—*e.g.*, in the paintings of the Cemetery of the Flavii at Tor Marancia—give good earnest of what was to follow, though it took time to bring it to perfection, so it is easy to detect in the most ancient classes of epitaphs manifest germs of the principal forms of epigraphy which prevailed in the second and third centuries.

Christian epigraphy perfected by degrees, but its general character shown from the first.

We have already selected some specimens from these classes as represented in Columns XVIII.-XX. of the Lateran Museum. We have seen that they were as short and simple as possible, often without a word beyond the name of the deceased, but also frequently whispering, as it were, gentle aspirations of Christian joy, hope, and charity, either in the emblems of the palm branch and the anchor, or in the words *Pax tibi*, *Pax tecum*. This is all that we read in the Cemetery of St. Priscilla. In those of Prætextatus and St. Agnes we find the same emblem

Simple, hopeful, and joyous.

Their Teaching about the Dead. 75

of hope, together with the symbol of faith, the mystical fish; also the same prayer for peace, together with another, somewhat more distinct perhaps, "Mayest thou live in God." If any one is disposed to feel disappointment at these phrases as too brief and meagre, he should remember that these three columns are made up of epitaphs upon the gravestones of men who died in the apostolic or immediately post-apostolic age.

If we turn to De Rossi's volume of dated inscriptions, we have seen that the same facts appear there also. Among the first thirty we have the fish and the anchor in the year 234; "Mayest thou live among the saints" in 268 [or 279]; *In pace*, A.D. 290; and prayers that the departed may be refreshed "with the holy souls," A.D. 291; or that "he may live in God," A.D. 307.

There are also other tokens of Christianity during the same period, such as these:—A man is said to have been taken to God, *receptus ad Deum*, A.D. 217; he is said to sleep, A.D. 249; to have received the grace of our Lord Jesus Christ, A.D. 268 [or 279]; and to have been fetched by the angels, A.D. 310.

And it is important that we should bear in mind (what has been already stated on De Rossi's irrefragable authority) that hardly one of these Christian *formulæ* (except *In pace*, which became extremely common, and in fact superseded all the rest) is to be found on the far more numerous inscriptions bearing later dates. All the tokens of the new religion which we have just mentioned from the gravestones of its professors fall within the compass of less than a hundred years before the accession of Constantine, during which period we have barely thirty dated inscriptions altogether; but whereas the next two centuries and a half (down to A.D. 590) give nearly fifteen hundred such inscriptions, yet, as we have said, not a single specimen occurs of the same simple, earnest, affectionate prayer for the departed as we have found during the first three centuries.

Less religious in fourth and later centuries.

The truth is, that during that early period those who dared to profess the Christian faith did so at the risk of their lives;

they valued it therefore as the pearl of great price, for the sake of which they hazarded the loss of all that they had, " counting all things to be but loss for the excellent knowledge of Jesus Christ their Lord."[1] When, therefore, they consigned some dear departed relative to the grave, they had no heart to record his worldly honours, his wisdom, or his talent; their thoughts were concentrated on his relations to God, and his condition in the new world into which he had just entered. They, therefore, either announced with confident assurance that his soul had been admitted to the happy lot reserved for the just who have left this world in peace; that he was united with the saints; that he was in God, and in the enjoyment of good things; or they breathed a humble and loving prayer that he might soon be admitted to a participation in these blessings. They asked for the departed soul peace, and light, and refreshment, and rest in God and in Christ. Sometimes also they invoked the help of his prayers (since they knew that he still lived in God) for the surviving relatives whose time of trial was not yet ended. In a word, they realised most intensely that all the faithful, whether in the body or out of the body, were still living members of one mystical body, the body of Christ; that they formed one great family, knit together in the closest bonds of love; and that this love, "stronger than death," had its proper work and happiness in prayer—prayer of the survivors for those who had gone before, prayer of the blessed for those who were left behind.

Life and love characteristics of the most ancient epitaphs.

By and by Christians became more numerous, but not more fervent; and now the warm expressions of a lively faith were heard more rarely. In most instances, they were exchanged for the cold conventionalities of a mere obituary record; and sometimes, as we have hinted, utterance is even given to sentiments more Pagan than Christian; such as, " Be of good courage, no man is immortal;" " Eternal sleep;" " Everlasting home" (in epitaphs of the years 356, 363, and 407); and one

Some exceptions, chiefly of later date.

[1] Philip. iii. 8.

even speaks of " malignant fortune having caused that the father *L.M.*, xv. 64; xvii. 10, 37, 40. should do for his son what the son ought rather to have done for his father." We do not say that these expressions must necessarily be understood in a sense absolutely inconsistent with the Christian faith, but certainly they are far from expressing the faith, or even savouring of it; they savour rather of the spirit and temper of the unbelieving world. But they are also manifestly exceptions to the general character of the epitaphs which were inscribed on the graves in the Catacombs. Of these, we repeat, the fundamental ideas are a firm belief in a future life, and a deep practical conviction that the division between this life and the next does not suffice to break the bonds of affection, nor to interrupt the interchange of kindly offices.

But before we produce the proofs of this from the epitaphs themselves of which we are treating, it will not be without its interest that we should briefly pass in review an episcopal instruction upon the subject, which was issued about the time to which a large number of these epitaphs belong, and of which they may reasonably be expected to be a tolerably faithful reflection.

Eusebius tells us that in the middle of the third century a pestilent disease took possession of many provinces of the world, and Africa was among the number of the provinces which suffered. Many Christians behaved with firm faith and true devotion under this trial, whilst others, either through weakness of mind or decay of faith, or because they were too much in love with the sweetness of this life or ill instructed in the truth, stood less steadily, and did not show forth that godlike and invincible courage which they should. *An episcopal instruction on death in the third century.*

Under these circumstances the Bishop of Carthage wrote a treatise, "De Mortalitate," and the burden of his discourse was this :—He insists that a true Christian ought to welcome death with joy, as introducing him to the port of his everlasting home and bestowing upon him immortality. "For this," he says, "is our peace, our trustworthy tranquillity, our sure, and firm, and everlasting security." "When the dear ones whom we love depart from the world, we ought rather to rejoice than grieve." "The present mortality may be a pestilence to the enemies of Christ, but to His servants it is a departure to salvation; by it the just are called away to refreshment (*refrigerium*), the unjust hurried off to punishment." He declares that God had often commanded him to be earnest and diligent in teaching that those of our brethren who are delivered from this world by the Divine summons (*accersitione*) ought not to be mourned for, because we know that they are not lost but only sent before (*non amitti, sed præmitti, recedentes præcedere*); that they should be desired indeed, but not bewailed; that we should not put on black garments for them here, when they have just put on white apparel there; that we should be careful not to give occasion to the Gentiles, who might justly find fault with us if we lament as extinct and lost those who, we say, are alive to God. "Eternal life cannot follow except first we have gone out [from this world]; it is not really a going out, but rather a passing over into eternity, when the journey of this life is ended. Let us then show ourselves to be in harmony with our creed, not grieving over the departure of those dear to us, and when the day of our own summons comes, going willingly and without delay to the Lord at His bidding. Heaven is our true country. Why then do we not make haste and run that we may come to it? A great number of our dear ones are expecting us there; a large assembly of parents, brothers, children is eagerly longing for us, assured of their own safety, anxious for ours. How great a joy both for us and for them that we should come to see and embrace them! How great a pleasure in that heavenly kingdom, where there is no more fear of dying! How high and enduring the happiness where there is eternity of living!"

Such was the teaching of St. Cyprian; now let us turn to the epitaphs. And, first, let us see what evidence they give

Their Teaching about the Dead. 79

of a belief in a future life, for this is the essential groundwork of the whole. It is contained in the very name given to their Christian burial-places—"cemeteries," or places for sleeping; in the name for death, "he sleeps;" and in the name for burial, *depositio*. About the two former phrases there will be no dispute; but the last is sometimes called in question, on the plea that it is not exclusively Christian, and passages are quoted from poets of the Augustan age who seem to use it in a similar sense. But it is one thing that the word should have been used two or three times by poets, whose choice of words is often determined, in part at least, by the exigencies of the metre, and quite another thing to find it repeated so incessantly upon Christian gravestones, that it came to be sufficiently represented by a single letter, or by two, DP or D. There is no really certain instance of its use in the same sense on any Pagan monuments. It is said, indeed, to have been found once in this abridged form, DP., on a Pagan sepulchre at Koppach in Austria, and once at full length on a monument in Rome; but in the first example, Mommsen suggests another reading; and, in the second, it does not stand alone, but is used in its purely classical sense of "placed," or "laid down." *Depositus P. XII. in vascello* is written on the monument—*i.e.*, the child was laid in some kind of urn or other vessel in the twelfth division[1] of the *columbarium*. Here it is simply equivalent to *situs*. But it cannot be fairly contended that this is its sense in the thousands of Christian inscriptions in which it stands alone on monuments of the third and fourth centuries. If so, we should have expected it to have been interchanged with other words having the same meaning, such as *situs* or *positus*, whereas these were not used till a later period. We therefore heartily endorse De Rossi's judgment that the word was intended to express the Christian truth that the body was only consigned to the earth for a while, as a sacred deposit which would be reclaimed at some future time when the sea and the earth shall give up their dead.

margin notes: Language of epitaphs denotes belief in future resurrection. Cemeteries; Sleep; Depositio. O.H., 6694. 4555.

[1] P[arte] or P[ariete], probably.

Their Teaching about the Dead.

1. To dear Cyriacus, sweetest son. Mayest thou live in the Holy Spirit.

2. Jesus Christ, Son of God, Saviour. To Pastor, a good and innocent son, who lived 4 years 5 months and 26 days. Vitalio and Marcellina, his parents.

3. In eternal sleep. Aurelius Gemellus, who lived ... years and 8 months and 18 days. His mother made this for her dearest well-deserving son. In peace. I commend [to thee], Bassilla, the innocence of Gemellus.

4. Lady Bassilla [= Saint Bassilla], we, Crescentinus and Micina, commend to thee our daughter Crescen[tina], who lived 10 months and ... days.

5. Matronata Matrona, who lived a year and 52 days. Pray for thy parents.

6. Anatolius made this for his well-deserving son, who lived 7 years 7 months and 20 days. May thy spirit rest well in God. Pray for thy sister.

7. Regina, mayest thou live in the Lord Jesus.

8. To my good and sweetest husband Castorinus, who lived 61 years 5 months and 10 days; well deserving. His wife made this. Live in God.

9. Amerimnus to his dearest well-deserving wife, Rufina. May God refresh thy spirit.

10. Sweet Faustina, mayest thou live in God.

11. Refresh, O God, the soul of ......

12. Bolosa, may God refresh thee, who lived 31 years; died on the 19th of September. In Christ.

13. Peace to thy soul, Oxycholis.

14. Agape, thou shalt live for ever.

15. In Christ. To Paulinus, a neophyte. In peace. Who lived 8 years.

16. Thy spirit in peace, Filumena.

17. In Christ. Æstonia, a virgin; a foreigner. Who lived 41 years and 8 days. She departed from the body on the 26th of February.

18. Victorina in peace and in Christ.

19. Dafnen, a widow, who whilst she lived burdened the Church in nothing.

20. To Leopardus, a neophyte, who lived 3 years 11 months. Buried on the 24th of March. In peace.

21. To Felix, their well-deserving son, who lived 23 years and 10 days; who went out of the world a virgin and a neophyte. In peace. His parents made this. Buried on the 2d of August.

22. Lucilianus to Bacius Valerius, who lived 9 years 8 [months] 22 days. A Catechumen.

82 *Epitaphs of the Catacombs.*

<small>Acclamations for the dead.</small>

Of the interchange of good offices between living Christians and the dead, the epitaphs in Column IX. of the Lateran Museum abound in proofs. We have printed on the preceding page a few specimens taken from photograph copies, and in explaining them we will give further illustrations of the subject from other examples, both in the Lateran Museum and elsewhere.

<small>(1) Of life in God.</small>

On Nos. 1, 7, 8, 10, and 14 of our selection we find the survivors praying for the deceased that he may live in God, or making a confident assertion that he does so live already, and will continue to do so for ever. In the Lateran there are eight or ten other specimens of the same kind in one or other of its forms, but we need not quote them. We cannot, however, omit one which was found some fifteen years since in one of the galleries near the Papal crypt in the Cemetery of St. Callixtus. All the gravestones near it were marked with anchors, ships, figures of the Good Shepherd, doves bearing the olive <small>*Bull.*, 1863, p. 82.</small> branch, and other symbols or phrases of the highest antiquity; and although the epitaph is longer than most of those written in the second or third centuries, both its Latinity, the classical form of the letters, and the religious phrase that is used in it, forbid us to assign it to any later date.

CHRE·SI·ME·DUL·CIS·SI·MA.ET·MI·HI·PI
EN·*tis·si*·MA·*fi·li·a·vi*·VAS·IN·DEO·QUE
RED·DE·DIT·ANN·V·M·VII·D:·V·CHRE·SI·MUS·ET
VI·CTO·RI·NA·PA·REN·T*es*·*VICTORIA*
VIVAS IN DEO

"Chresime, my sweetest and most affectionate daughter, mayest thou live in God, who gave up [her soul] at the age of five years seven months and five days. Chresimus and Victorina, her parents. *Victoria, mayest thou live in God.*"

It is evident that the deceased child had the names of both her parents, and the stone had been first cut according to the instructions of the father, who addressed her by the name she had received from him, Chresima. Then the salutation of the

Their Teaching about the Dead. 83

mother, calling her Victoria, and repeating the acclamation, was added by another hand; it was probably dictated by the mother herself, as the fossor was closing the grave.

Nos. 6, 13, 16, and 18 predicate or petition peace for the (2) Peace. departed, and the same comforting word is not omitted from others also, Nos. 15 and 21. In Column IX. at the Lateran we read, "Peace to thy soul, Zosima;" "Saturnina sleeps in peace;" "Lais, with peace;" "May thy spirit rest in good;" Nos. 29, 35. 15. and immediately outside the gate of the gallery, at the head of the staircase, is a whole class of inscriptions from the Cœmeterium Ostrianum, consisting simply of the name of the deceased, followed by this formula:—*Attica in pace, Romano in pace, Gaiane in pace, Ireneo in pace, Dextra in pace, Istercorio benemerenti te in pace*, &c., &c.

Another acclamation, of which we have given some examples (3) Refreshin Nos. 9, 11, and 12, asks for refreshment for the deceased; ment. and in an epitaph of the Kircherian Museum we read, "Kalemere, may God refresh thy spirit, together with that of thy sister Hilare;" and in the Vatican,

    ΗΡΑΚΛΙΑ ΡΩΜΗ
    [Ε]ΙC ΑΝΑΠΑΥCΙΝ
    COY Η ΨΥΧΗ
    "Heraclia Roma, thy soul into refreshment."

Nobody can fail to recognise the substantial identity of the episcopal instruction and the popular creed. Not only do the same thoughts and sentiments pervade both, but in many instances they are expressed by the same words. With St. Cyprian, to die is "to be summoned by God," "to go out of this world," "to retire," and "to go before." The dead "live to God," are gone to "peace" and "refreshment;" and every one of these words and phrases occur more or less frequently on the tombstones. St. Cyprian, indeed, does not speak of the living making supplication for these blessings for the dead; for the motive of his writing led him rather to insist on the certain blessedness of the dead; but he speaks of the dead who are thus secure as to their own salvation, being still anxious about ours, and this, of course, lies at the foundation of the prayers which the survivors were in the habit of addressing to them for the charity of their assistance.

<small>These phrases explained.</small>

We will return to these presently, but first let us say a few words about the origin and meaning of each of the formulæ that we have seen used on behalf of the dead, and let us show how they were the natural and legitimate fruit of Christian doctrine and belief. And first of life. To a Pagan mourner, smarting under some bitter bereavement, it would have seemed the most heartless mockery to speak of life as still present, or to ask for it as a gift presently to be bestowed, just at the moment when it had been taken away. On the other hand, nothing could be more natural than that the Christian should thus intimately unite the thoughts of life and death. Our blessed Lord, when raising Lazarus from the dead, had declared that He was Himself "the Resurrection and the Life." "He that believeth in Me, although he be dead, shall live, and every one that liveth and believeth in Me shall not die for ever." Christians were taught that, by virtue of their baptism, they had "put on Christ;" that though "dying, yet behold they live;" that in this world they were "already dead, and their life was hid with Christ in God."[1] This hidden life of the soul was alone worthy of the name of life, and the death of the body did not destroy but perfect it. When that event should happen, then that part of them which had heretofore been corruptible would put on incorruption, and what had been mortal would put on immortality; the body would only exchange one life which was fleeting and miserable for another which was higher and better and more enduring. We have proof in the "Acts of the Martyrs" that such thoughts were present to their minds when they were brought near to death; and doubtless they were present also to those who buried the dead. "Offer sacrifice to the gods," said the Heathen magistrate to St. Julius, "and you shall live with us." "To live with you," was the spirited reply, "would be to die; but when I shall have died, then I live." "You are determined then

<small>Life.</small>

---

[1] St. John xi. 25; Gal. iii. 27; 2 Cor. vi. 9; Coloss. iii. 3.

Their Teaching about the Dead. 85

to die, and not to live," retorted the magistrate. "I choose to die temporarily that I may live eternally."[1]

But the Christian epitaphs asked not only for life but also Refreshment. for "refreshment" (*refrigerium*). This is a word which may be found in some Pagan epitaphs, not in the sense of a gift asked for the dead, but as an invitation to the living to partake of bodily refreshment in a repast. *Refrigeri sine bile* is part of a long Pagan inscription to the memory of one Aurelius Vitalis, who built a monument for the burial of himself and relatives *R.S.*, iii. and a few special friends, whom he invited to assemble together at his tomb whilst they lived, and there to take refreshment, eating and drinking in peace and harmony with one another. And as the joys of heaven are often represented in Holy Scripture under the figure of a feast, some persons would interpret the word in the same sense when it occurs on Christian epitaphs or in the "Acts of the Martyrs"—*e.g.*, in the "Acts of St. Perpetua," who saw in a vision her brother *refrigerantem*—*i.e.* (as they interpret), seated at the heavenly banquet. Others, however, insist upon understanding it in this place as merely "refreshed" in opposition to the heat and thirst from which he had been previously suffering ; as, also, when St. Maximus of Turin, in one of his sermons on St. Laurence, opposed the *refrigerium* promised in the kingdom of heaven to the fiery torments which that saint suffered in his martyrdom. The Psalmist seems to use it as a synonym for relief from distress and difficulty in general, as when he says, "Thou hast brought us into a net. Thou hast laid affliction on our back ; we have passed through fire and water, and Thou hast brought us out into a refreshment" (Ps. lxv. 11) ; and perhaps the ancient Christians used it also in the same wide sense, as expressing the cessation of all evil and the enjoyment of all good.

Whatever may have been the precise meaning which they attached to the word, there is abundant evidence that it was familiar to them in connection with their thoughts and prayers for the dead. Tertullian uses it at the very beginning of the

[1] Acta Sincera, Ruinart, tom. iii. p. 273.

third century in his account of the devotions of a widow praying for her deceased husband. "She prays for his soul," he says,[1] "asks for refreshment for him, and for herself a share with him in the first resurrection, and she offers [sacrifice] for him on the anniversary of his death." St. Paulinus, of Nola, writing to his dear friend Amandus,[2] announces to him the death of his brother, concerning whom he expresses a fear that he has gone out of this world "a debtor" to God; whereupon he entreats Amandus to unite with him in the labour of prayer "that the merciful God may through your prayers refresh his soul with the drops of His mercy. For as the fire enkindled by Him will burn even to the lowest hell,[3] so without doubt the dew of His pardon will penetrate to Hades (*infera*), so that those who are suffering there in the burning darkness may be refreshed by the dew and light of His pity."

The same language was consecrated to Christian ears by its use in the most ancient Liturgies—*e.g.*, in a prayer that "Christ will, through the intercession of His holy martyrs, grant to our dear ones who sleep in Him refreshment in the abode of the living;"[4] or another, "that the prayers of the blessed martyrs will so commend us to Christ that He will grant eternal refreshment to our dear ones who sleep in Him;" and there are other petitions also to the same effect.[5]

In pace.

Other epitaphs that we have seen prayed for peace, or predicated that the deceased is already in the enjoyment of peace. The precise meaning of this, as of the last, has been the subject of much controversy. Where it is predicated of the deceased, some authors understand it in the same sense as the word is used by Tertullian, St. Cyprian,[6] and other of the earliest Fathers—viz., as denoting communion with the Church. And

[1] De Monog, c. x.   [2] Epist. xx. p. 191, ed. Antwerp, 1622.
[3] Deut. xxxii. 22.   [4] Muratori, Liturg. Rom., t. ii. pp. 652, 653.
[5] Some authors have illustrated these prayers for *refrigerium* by reference to one or two Pagan epitaphs in which Osiris is invoked to give cold water to the deceased. O. H., 4766. Fabretti, p. 465, xix. Mus. Veron. 3183. But there is no trace of this Orientalism in the inscriptions of the Catacombs.
[6] St. Cyprian, De Lapsis, cc. xv. xxxiii.; Tertull., De Virg. Vel., c. ii., De Pudic., c. xii.

Their Teaching about the Dead. 87

it cannot be doubted that in the Christian inscriptions which have come to us from Africa this interpretation is correct. But in these, as we have already seen, the word is coupled with life, not with death; it follows the verb *vixit;* that is to say, it is not asserted concerning the deceased that he sleeps in peace now, neither is it made a subject of prayer that he may enjoy peace hereafter, but it is said that he has lived in peace for so many years and months, and this can only be understood of the peace and communion of Holy Church.

Others have preferred to see in this peace, when predicated of the dead, a reference to the troubles and sufferings of Christians during life, from which the peace of death was a happy deliverance. And more than one passage might be quoted from the Jewish Scriptures[1] which would seem to countenance such an interpretation. Moreover, we are told[2] that in the calendars of the Greek Church these words are used to distinguish confessors from martyrs, those saints who died a natural death from those who had sealed their testimony with their blood; just as the Prophet Jeremias uses *in pace* in opposition to *in gladio*, saying, "Thou shalt not die by the sword, but thou shalt die in peace."[3] No doubt, therefore, this would be a very natural use of the word; yet it can hardly be accepted as an adequate explanation of it, as it was understood by the early Christians when they inscribed it on their gravestones. It cannot be doubted that they had present to their minds the peace of a joyful resurrection and happy eternity; not, indeed, excluding all idea of that peace and reconciliation with God which is to be enjoyed in this world as a prelude and preparation for the other, yet at the same time not always thinking of this peace or expressly alluding to it; or rather thinking of them united together, as St. Cyprian did when he wrote concerning heretics,[4] "They cannot arrive at the reward

---

[1] Ecclus. xliv. 11.; Wisdom iii. 3.
[2] Scacchius de Not. et Sign. Sanct., c. ix. 2.
[3] Jer. xxxiv. 5; cf. Gen. xv. 15; 4 Kings xxii. 20.
[4] De Unit. Eccles. xi. in fin.

of peace who have broken the peace of the Lord by the madness of discord." Arnobius, too, writing about the same time, couples it with pardon of sins, and says distinctly that we ask for it both for the living and the dead :—*Pax et venia a nobis postulatur . . . et adhuc vitam degentibus et resolutis corporum vinctione.*[1]

Good.

In one of the inscriptions which we quoted just now from Column IX. of the Lateran Collection (No. 15), there was a prayer that the spirit of the deceased (Lais) might rest in good, *in bono*, and the same phrase is to be seen in many other epitaphs both of the same and of other collections. We may still read in the mortar round one of the graves in the Catacomb of St. Alexander on the Via Nomentana, *Saviniane, Spiritus tu(u)s in bono;* Boldetti gives us another, *Salonice, Ispiritus tu(u)s in bonu;* Marangoni a third,[2] *Attice, Spiritus tu(u)s in bonu;* and others have been preserved in books not so easily accessible. Some persons take *bonum* in these epitaphs as being simply equivalent to God, the one Supreme Good, just as the evil from which we pray to be delivered at the end of the Lord's Prayer may be understood as standing for the Evil one himself, as well as for all other minor forms of evil. *Suscipe servum tuum in bonum* is a prayer of the Royal Psalmist (Ps. cxviii. 122); and in another Psalm he says, "His soul shall dwell in good things" (xxiv. 13). M. Le Blant quotes an ancient commentator on this Psalm (Cassiodorus) as saying that the word "good things" is here used, because the just do not on leaving this life at once receive the complete happiness promised to the saints after the resurrection; and yet, through the confident expectation they have of receiving one day that fulness of reward, they already "dwell in good;" they are in a state of enjoyment through the foretaste of the judgment that is to come. And M. Le Blant believes that in like manner the word *bonum* was used in these epitaphs as furnishing by its indefiniteness a convenient cloak for the uncertainty in which men's minds were

p. 418.

ii. p. 406.

[1] Adversus gentes, lib. iv. c. 36.   [2] Acta Sti. Victorini, p. 119.

then fluctuating as to the condition of departed souls in the interval between death and the general resurrection. This uncertainty is clearly testified by the words of St. Augustine[1] about his departed friend Nebridius, where he says that "he is now in Abraham's bosom, whatever the place may be that ought to be understood by that word." St. Gregory Nazianzus expresses the same doubt; and, of course, many and weighty names of the first few centuries might be quoted in favour of believing that the souls even of the blessed were detained in an intermediate state of expectation until the time of "the first resurrection." It is remarkable, however, that no trace of this doctrine is to be found in the Christian epitaphs of Rome, which must certainly have been a faithful reflection of the popular belief upon the subject, and we see no reason therefore for adopting M. Le Blant's explanation of *in bono*. The general tenor of the epitaphs in the Catacombs is strongly against it; sometimes (one is almost tempted to think) designedly so—*e.g.*,

PRIMA VIVIS IN GLORIA DEI ET IN PACE DOMINI NOSTRI.

"Prima, thou livest in the glory of God, and in the peace of our Lord Jesus Christ."[2]

He seems disposed to extend the same interpretation to another phrase which was sometimes used—viz., *cum sanctis*, *inter sanctos*—because St. Paul teaches[3] that the saints, "though approved by faith, yet have not yet received the promise, God providing some better thing for us, that they should not be perfected without us." But without entering into any discussion as to the full meaning of this text, we think it cannot be doubted that the general tone of the most ancient Christian epitaphs is more in harmony with such a picture as is drawn by St. Paulinus of Nola, for example,[4] who represents a whole host

Inter sanctos, *R.S.*, ii. xlv., 18: i. xxiii., 9.

---

[1] Confess., ix. 3.
[2] Scratched in the mortar round a grave in the lower part of the Cemetery of Thraso.—Marangoni, Acta Sti. Victorini, p. 69.
[3] Heb. xi. 39, 40.   [4] Natal., vi. 140.

of the saints going forth from heaven to receive the soul of St Felix as soon as it had left the body, and conducting it in triumph before the throne of God. This is certainly the thought which dictated the following epitaph :—

Bull., 1875, p. 19.

   PAULO FILIO MERENTI IN PA
   CEM TE SUSCIPIAN OMNIUM ISPIRI
   TA SANCTORUM QUI VIXIT ANNOS II. DIES N. L.

This epitaph has been already quoted in another connection (p. 25), but it may be repeated here for the sake of the illustration it gives to our present subject. We desire also to point out its striking resemblance to the language of the Ritual, which, as the dead body is taken up to be carried from the church to the grave, breaks forth into a most plaintive yet inspiring acclamation, " May the angels lead thee into Paradise; may the martyrs receive thee (*suscipiant te*) at thy approach, and lead thee to the holy city Jerusalem. May the choir of angels receive thee, and mayest thou have eternal rest with Lazarus, who was once poor."

This last phrase is of course equivalent to a mention of Abraham's bosom, and corresponds to the prayers of some of the early martyrs—*e.g.*, of SS. Tryphon and Respicius, A.D. 250, who prayed in the midst of their torments, " Lord Jesus, receive our souls, and place them in the bosom of Thy patriarchs."[1] But it is most especially in the liturgies that we shall find the originals of all these prayers and aspirations for the dead, so that De Rossi justly calls them the very echo of the prayers of the liturgy. Of one inscription in particular—

Agreement of these prayers with those of the liturgies.

R.S., ii. 305.

   IN PACE SPIRITUS SILVANI, AMEN,

he says, one seems to " hear in it the last words of the funeral rites, just as the tomb is being closed and the sorrowing survivors bid farewell to the grave." And we may almost say the same of another, set up to the memory of a child who died when five years old, and of her father, who died the following

---

[1] Acta Sincera, tom. i. 375.

day. Nothing is added but the words *Suscipiantur in pace*. R.S., iii. 126.
But indeed it is scarcely possible to name a single formula used
in these epitaphs—unless it be something perfectly exceptional
—which is absent from the ancient liturgies; and, contrariwise,
almost all the prayers for the dead in our liturgical books find
their germ at least, if not their exact prototype, on the gravestones of the Catacombs. Thus, when we bury the dead, we
pray that "henceforth they may live to God." In the Canon
of the Mass we pray daily, " Remember, O Lord, Thy servants
who have gone before us, and who sleep in the sleep of peace;"
and if we go down into the Catacombs of SS. Nereus and
Achilles we read the same memento on the old gravestones
that are lying there.

ΑΥΡ. ΑΙΔΙΑΝΟC ΠΑΦΛΑΓΩΝ ΘΕΟΥ ΔΟΥΛΟC ΠΙCΤΟC
ΕΚΟΙΜΗΘΗ ΕΝ ΕΙΡΗΝΗ ΜΝΗCΘΗ ΑΥΤΟΥ Ο ΘΕΟC ΕΙC ΤΟΥC
ΑΙΩΝΑC

"Aurelius Ælianus of Paphlagonia, a faithful servant of God, sleeps in peace. May God remember him for ever."

ΔΗΜΗΤΡΙC ΕΤ ΛΕΟΝΤΙΑ CΒΙΡΙΚΕ ΦΕΙΛΙΕ
ΒΕΝΕΜΕΡΤΙ ΜΝΗCΘΗC ΙΗCΟΥC Ο ΚΥΡΙΟC ΤΕΚΝΟΝ.

"Demetrius and Leontia to their well-deserving daughter, Sirica. Lord Jesus, remember our child."

The prayer in the Canon of the Mass runs on, "Grant to
them, O Lord, and to all who are at rest in Christ, a place of
refreshment, light, and peace;" or, as it is more fully expressed
in a special prayer for all the dead lying in any cemetery, "Grant
them a place of refreshment, the blessedness of rest, and clear-
ness of light;" or in another special prayer on the anniversary of a death, "Place them in a region of peace and light, and
bid them be partakers in the lot of Thy saints."

The only petition in these collects of the Church of which Prayers for
we have not seen examples from the Catacombs is that for light.
light; and even this has been found in the Cemetery of St.
Callixtus. De Rossi has placed it among the rarer class of

epitaphs (*dictionis singularis*) in Column XVII. at the Lateran. It runs thus :—

xvii. 14.

DOMINE NE QUANDO ADUMBRETUR SPIRITUS
VENERES DE FILIUS IPSEIUS QUI SUPERSTI
TIS SUNT BENIROSUS PROJECTUS.

"O Lord, let not the spirit of Venera be in darkness—Of her sons who survive, Venerosus and Projectus."

This petition for light may have been suggested to the early Christians by the language which they heard around them coupling death and darkness together. Thus a Pagan mother says on the epitaph of her son that he had enjoyed the hospitable light (*hospitio lucis*) for thirty-eight years, but that now a dark day has carried him off from the light and buried him in bitter death. "Traveller, curse me not as you pass, for I am in darkness and cannot answer," says another Heathen inscription; and a third, "Here I lie, unhappy girl, in darkness." And sometimes they set up lamps at the tombs of their friends, accompanied by the most earnest and pathetic appeals that they might be kept always burning. On the other hand, light is often spoken of in the New Testament as belonging in a special way to the Christian dispensation, and an essential characteristic of its Divine Founder. His forerunner had said of Him, "In Him was life, and the life was the light of men;" and He said of Himself, "I am the light of the world; he that followeth me walketh not in darkness, but shall have the light of life."[1] Hence, it was the practice of the ancient Christians every evening at the lighting of the lamps to give thanks to God for the gift of faith whereby their souls were enlightened.[2] Thus on several accounts, whether we consider the natural darkness of the grave and the impenetrable gloom in which it was shrouded to the Pagan mind, or whether we take light as

O.H., 7375.
Gruter, 923, 5.

Muratori, 1384, 7.

O.H., 4838; 4416.
I.R.N., 166.
C.I.L., 1.2102.

Bull., 1867, p. 14; 1868, p. 78.

---
[1] St. John i. 4; viii. 12.
[2] See the Greek Evening Hymn, iii. in Daniel's *Thesaurus Hymnologicus*, t. iii. p. 5; also Prudentius, *Cathemerin.*, *Hymn V. ad incensum Cerei.*

Their Teaching about the Dead. 93

another name for grace and mercy, as in the Psalms,[1] or as an emblem of faith, or, lastly, as a synonym for Christ Himself, we can understand why this too should have entered into the petitions of Christians for their dead. God dwells in light inaccessible, and what faith does for the living the presence of God does yet more perfectly for those who have penetrated within the veil; and hence in the famous ancient epitaph of Autun we find Christ directly addressed by this title of Light of the dead.

ET ETΔOI MHTHP CE ΛITAZOMAI ΦΩC TO ΘANONTΩN.

"May my mother rest well, I pray Thee, O Light of the dead."

We have seen St. Cyprian instructing his people that the dead who are at rest in the Lord enjoy a sense of blessed security indeed for themselves and their own salvation, but are solicitous for those whom they have left behind; and hence in the epitaph which stands as No. 5 in our selection, an infant is asked to pray for her parents; in No. 6 a child of seven is bid to pray for his sister; in another, the foster parents of a lady who has died at the age of thirty or thirty-six[2] call upon her to pray for her husband, Celsinianus.

Prayers to the saints.

AURELIVS AGAPETVS ET AURELIA
FELICISSIMA ALVMNE FELICITATI
DIGNISSIMÆ QVE VICSIT ANIS XXX ET VI
ET PETE PRO CELSINIANV COJVGEM.

L. M., viii. 12.

To which we may add another from the Cemetery of St. Callixtus:—

VINCENTIA IN ☧ PETAS PRO PHŒBE ET PRO VIRGINIO EJUS.

"Vincentia in Christ. Pray for Phœbe and her husband."

In other instances, there is no blood relationship between the

---

[1] See Bellarmine in Ps. xlii.
[2] It is not improbable that M. (menses) was accidentally omitted after VI., and that she was only 30½ when she died.

94   *Epitaphs of the Catacombs.*

deceased and those who ask his prayers; but he is "an innocent child," and is now "with the saints," and therefore "the man who composed his epitaph and the man who carved it beg to be "remembered in his holy prayers." (The original is in the Kircherian Museum).

ΔΙΟΝΤCΙΟC ΝΗΠΙΟC ΑΚΑΚΟC ΕΝΘΑΔΕ
ΚΕΙΤΕ ΜΕΤΑ ΤΩΝ ΑΓΙΩΝ ΜΝΗCΚΕCΘΕ
ΔΕ ΚΑΙ ΗΜΩΝ ΕΝ ΤΑΙC ΑΓΙΑΙC ΥΜΩΝ
ΠΡΕΥΧΑΙC ΚΑΙ ΤΟΥ ΓΑΤΨΑ [Ν] ΤΟC ΚΑΙ
ΓΡΑΨΑΝΤΟC.

At other times the request for prayers is general, and no special plea is urged, as in the following, the first of which comes from the Cemetery of St. Callixtus; the second from the Cemetery of Thraso, on the Via Salaria Nova; the next two may still be seen in the Cemetery of SS. Nereus and Achilles; and the last have been preserved to us by Boldetti.

R.S., iii.; Tav.,
xxviii., 22.
Bull, 1873, p. 71.

(1.)   JANUARIA BENE REFRIGERA ET ROGA PRO NOS

(2.)   SOZON BENEDICTUS
                  REDIDIT AN NOBE
                  BERUS[1] ☧ ISPIRUM
                  IN PACE ET PET PRONOBIS.

(3.)   ...VIBAS IN PACE ET PET PRO NOBIS.

(4.)   ZHCAIC EN KΩ ΚΑΙ ΕΡΩΤΑ ΥΠΕΡ ΗΜΩΝ.

p. 418.   (5.) JOVIANE, VIBAS IN DEO ET ROG...

p. 490.   (6.) SABBATI, DULCIS ANIMA, ROGA ET PETE.

(1.) Januaria, mayest thou be well refreshed, and pray for us.

(2.) Sozon Benedictus died at the age of nine years. May the real Christ receive thy spirit in peace; and pray for us.

(3.) Mayest thou live in peace, and pray for us.

(4.) Mayest thou live in the Lord, and pray for us.

(5.) Jovianus, mayest thou live in God, and pray...

(6.) Sabbatius, sweet soul, ask and pray...

Of these formulas, *pete pro nobis* was used so frequently that

---

[1] *Verus* seems used here against the Marcionite heresy, which taught that Christ was no reality, but only an appearance: whence Tertullian wrote on the *vera caro* of Christ. At a later period, *Verus Deus* would rather have been insisted upon.

Their Teaching about the Dead. 95

it is found abbreviated into the mere initial letters, either of its words or syllables, P.P.N., or PT.P.NB.; just as on Pagan inscriptions DD. is put for *dedicat*, BNM. for *benemerenti*, MM. for *memoriæ*, PP. for *perpetuus* or *præpositus*, and even QD. for *quondam*.

C.I.I., iii., p. 1185.

If we were writing a theological treatise or forging weapons of controversy, it would be necessary to enter into many further particulars about these inscriptions; but we have now said enough for our present purpose, which is only to set before our readers a fair account of the most ancient Christian epitaphs taken as a whole. We have called attention to their chief characteristics, and the contrast between their life, hope, and cheerfulness and the cold despondency or the defiant wrath of the inscriptions on Pagan sepulchres has been brought out sufficiently.

We will only add a word as to the value that ought to be attached to the interchange of prayers between the living and the dead, of which we have seen so many examples. It is sometimes said that they were no real acts of faith, hope, or charity, no religious acts at all, but the mere senseless outpourings of natural affection, differing in form only, and accidentally rather than substantially, from the Pagan acclamations that the earth might lie lightly on their dead. It is said that they were dictated by the heart rather than the head, and probably proceeded from the less instructed portion of the Christian community.

The religious value of these prayers,

It seems hard to see on what plea the merit of a religious act can be denied to such an inscription as the following:—

LUCIFERE COJUGI DULCISSIME OMNEM
DULCITUDINEM CUM LUCTUM MAXIME
MARITO RELIQUIT, ET MERUIT TITULUM
INSCRIBI UT QUISQUI DE FRATRIBUS LEGERIT ROGET DEU
UT SANCTO ET INNOCENTI SPIRITO AD DEUM SUSCIPIATUR.

I..M., ix. 10.

"To my sweetest wife Lucifera, who was all sweetness,[1] whereas she

---
[1] Where there is such flagrant violation of all rules of grammar, we can only translate according to the most probable conjecture of the meaning.

left to her husband the greatest sorrow, and she has deserved that an epitaph should be inscribed to her, to the end that whosoever of the brethren shall read it may ask God that her holy and innocent spirit may be received to God."

On a corner of the gravestone it is written in smaller letters that this lady died at the early age of twenty-two years, four months, and ten days. No doubt the widower's epitaph is dictated by the heart; it is the expression of sorrowing love; but it is also, to our seeming at least, an act of piety and faith; and the writer asks his brethren to do precisely that act of religion on behalf of his wife which we find from scores of examples that they were in the continual habit of doing for those who were nearest and dearest to them.

<small>and their orthodoxy.</small>

And as to the invocation of the martyrs being an unauthorised act of devotion, common only to the ignorant, it will be sufficient perhaps to quote the conclusion of Pope Damasus' inscription in honour of St. Agnes, which Marangoni[1] was fortunate enough to rescue from destruction when it was already in the masons' hands, and which still survives in the wall by which we descend to her Basilica *fuori le mura*. In it the Pope, after invoking her as an object of veneration, a distinguished martyr, and the glory of Christian modesty, begs her to lend a favourable ear to his prayers. What more or what less was asked of their departed friends by the more humble writers of the several epitaphs we have quoted above?

<small>*L.M.*, iii. 1.</small>

O VENERANDA MIHI SANCTUM DECUS ALMA PUDORIS
UT DAMASI PRECIBUS FAVEAS PRECOR INCLYTA MARTYR.

[1] Acta Sti. Victorini, p. 137.

CHAPTER VI.

DOGMATIC ALLUSIONS.

Unreasonable to look for an exposition of Christian doctrine in epitaphs, yet some allusions to it may be expected—This expectation realised with reference to belief in one God, in Christ and in the Holy Ghost—Some peculiar phrases with reference to the Holy Trinity—Devotion to the Saints.

THE inscriptions engraved on ordinary tombstones in the Catacombs are necessarily short, so that they often contain little more than what is of the very essence of such documents—viz., the name of the deceased. But even if there had been no such narrow limits to the space that might be used, yet it would not have been reasonable to expect from them any complete enunciation of the articles of the Christian faith. It might naturally have been expected that some of those articles would be alluded to, especially those which had reference to the present condition or future prospects of the dead; and here, as we have seen, there is no reason to complain of their silence; but it would be ridiculous to look for anything like a formal statement of the whole Christian Creed. {Unreasonable to look for the creed in Christian epitaphs.}

It was necessary to premise this remark, because it has been sometimes attempted to draw inferences hostile to certain doctrines of the Catholic faith from the supposed silence of early Christian epitaphs about them, as though it were usual to find a full profession of a man's creed upon his tombstone. On the other hand, we should have a right to be greatly astonished if it were not possible, from a collection of several thousands of sepulchral inscriptions belonging to men and women professing the same religion, to gather some idea, more or less {Yet some allusions to it may be expected.}

G

distinct, of some of the principal tenets and characteristics of that religion. Let us inquire, therefore, what information we can gain from the epitaphs of the Roman Catacombs as to the object of Christian worship.

Epitaphs of the Catacombs show belief in one God.

Bull., 1877, p. 25.

At the head of this series De Rossi places a few epitaphs which bear the title (so to call it) of "the name of God;" this being, as he rightly calls it, the initial formula of every solemn Christian act, because the Christian religion is essentially the worship of the one true God, in opposition to the doctrines of polytheism. Hence, in some of the edicts of the Emperors who persecuted the Church, this is the very name and title by which the Christians are called, "men who confess themselves to be worshippers of God." On the same principle Lactantius calls the Christian religion *Religio Dei* and *Lex Dei;* and the Pagan Symmachus, intending to say that a large number of the citizens of Benevento are Christian, thinks it sufficient to say that "they worship God."

Bull., 1863, p. 59.

De Rossi has found a very ancient *graffito* in St. Callixtus, saying *Mensurius in Deu credidit,* "Mensurius believed in God;" and Boldetti gives another inscription which seems to speak still more precisely, and says that such an one "believed in one God" (*In unu Deu credidit*). St. Ambrose, however, and other authors, tell us that from time immemorial the Roman Church always recited the creed without the addition of this word *Unum,* so that we are led to suspect either that this particular person was a stranger in Rome, familiar with the formularies of another country, or else perhaps that he had taken part in some of the dogmatic controversies of his day,

Bull., 1866, p. 80. R.S., ii. 303.

In Christ.

and distinguished himself in some way by his defence of the unity of the Godhead.

But though the unity of the Godhead was the fundamental doctrine of Christianity as opposed to the polytheistic worship of the Heathen, it was known to the faithful themselves, and even to the Pagans—witness the famous letter of Pliny—that they also worshipped Christ as God. Hence they wrote also on their inscriptions, "In the name of Christ," "In God the Lord Christ," or "In God Christ." And in the Cemetery of St. Callixtus, which was more immediately under the supervision of the Bishop, they wrote with a closer adherence to the orthodox formularies of faith, and, indeed, the very words of all the ancient creeds, "In God and in Christ." The omission of the conjunction might, under critical circumstances, have given just cause of offence and suspicion of unsoundness in the faith, as giving countenance to the heresy of Noetus and the Patripassians. There could be no such apprehension as to the Catholic faith of the writers of the following epitaphs, all of which come from the cemetery of the Popes themselves :— *L.M.*, viii. 3, 4, 8, 10.

    AUGURINE IN DOM ET ☧   *R.S.*, ii. xxxix. 30; xxvii. 52.

    PAX DOM ET ☧
    CUM FAUSTIN[O] ATTICO

    ΓΕΝΕϹΙ   xlvii. 52.
    ϹΤΙΝΑ Η ΕΝ ΘΕΩ ΚΑΙ ΧΡΙϹΤΩ ΠΙϹΤΕΥϹΑϹ   xliii. 39.
    Ϲ ΤΟΙϹ ΑΝΓΕΛΟΙϹ

It is much to be regretted that only a fragment of the last epitaph should have reached us. Enough, however, is preserved to show that Faustina was one who believed in God and Christ; and in the two others there is the same distinct enumeration of the two First Persons of the Blessed Trinity.

Occasionally the early Christians wrote D.M. ☧ S., as though they would Christianise the ordinary Pagan form of dedication to the *Dî Manes* by introducing into it the name of Christ. This formula may be read as equivalent to either *Domino Christo Sacrum*, according to the ancient practice of writing the initials of syllables,[1] or to *Deo Magno Christo Sacrum*, or more probably *Deo Magno Christo Salvatori*, according to the words of St. Paul in his Epistle to Titus,[2] where he speaks of "the great God and our Saviour Jesus Christ." *Bull.*, 1873, p. 129.

Then, again, they often placed the word ΙΧΘΥϹ at the beginning or end of their epitaphs, not as part of a sentence,

---
[1] See p. 95.   [2] Chap. ii. 13.

but as a complete formula in itself; and our readers need not be told how this was equivalent to a declaration of faith in "Jesus Christ, Son of God, Saviour." We have given an example of this kind of inscription in No. 2 of our selection in page 80, and other examples may be seen both in the Lateran and Kircherian Museums in Rome. One in the latter collection has a remarkable variation of the formula, too significant to be passed over in silence. The epitaph in question was found in our own time in the ancient Cemetery of the Vatican, and belongs to the end of the second or beginning of the third century. It is ornamented at the top by a wreath; then follow the letters D.M., and in the next line ΙΧΘΥC ΖΩΝΤΩΝ. Below this are two fishes, one on either side of an anchor, followed by an inscription which is unhappily incomplete.

Bull., 1870, p. 50.

LICINIÆ AMIATI BENE
MERENTI VIXIT

But it is clear that the phrase ιχθύς ζώντων stood alone, as the ιχθύς does in other epitaphs; and when we call to mind the hidden meaning of the word taken alone, we can only understand "*Fish of the living*," inscribed on a memorial of the dead, as having reference to those words of our Lord, "He that believeth in Me, although he be dead, shall live; every one that believeth in Me shall not die for ever," for "God is not the God of the dead but of the living."[1]

and in the Holy Ghost.

Nor is the Third Person of the Blessed Trinity absent from these epitaphs. If we read on some stones "In Christ" or "In the name of Christ," we read on another (in the Kircherian Museum), "In the Holy Spirit of God." ΠΡΩΤΟΣ ΕΝ ΑΓΙΩ ΠΝΕΥΜΑΤΙ ΘΕΟΥ ΕΝΘΑΔΕ ΚΕΙΤΑΙ ΦΙΡΜΙΑΛΑ ΑΔΕΛΦΗ ΜΝΗΜΗΣ ΧΑΡΙΝ. "Protus, in the Holy Spirit of God, is buried here. His sister Firmilla [set this up] for remembrance' sake." As the survivors prayed for their deceased relatives that they might live "in God," or "in Christ," "in God Christ," or "in

[1] St. John, xi. 25, 26; St. Matt. xxii. 32.

Dogmatic Allusions. 101

the Lord Jesus," so also they sometimes prayed, "Mayest thou live in the Holy Spirit: *Car Kuriaco Fil dulcissimo Vibas (i)n Spirito san.*[1] The same formula probably occurs in another *R.S.*, ii. xliii. 32. epitaph also, though its present fragmentary condition does not allow us to speak with certainty.

PAULUS EVOCHIATI
[IN] SPIRITO SANCTO

The Holy Spirit is also mentioned in an epitaph of the end of the second century, which has been already quoted, in which God is said to have recalled to Himself the soul of a girl about ten years old, *Spiritu sancto suo castam pudicam et inviolabilem semper—i.e.,* that had always been kept chaste, modest, and inviolate through the influence of His Holy Spirit. And De Rossi illustrates this by another, which was dug up near the Via Latina some twenty years ago. Several of its phrases savour of great antiquity, and in fact he himself calls it *antiquissima*.

ΙΟΤΛΕΙΑΣ ΕΤΑΡΕΣΤΑΣ   *I.C.*, cxvi.
ΤΗΣ ΘΕΟΦΙΛΕΣΤΑΤΗΣ
Η ΣΑΡΞ ΕΝΘΑΔΕ ΚΕΙΤΑΙ
ΨΤΧΗ ΔΕ ΑΝΑΚΑΙΝΘΕΙΣΑ
ΤΩ ΠΝΕΤΜΑΤΙ ΧΡΙΣΤΟΤ
ΚΑΙ ΑΓΓΕΛΙΚΟΝ ΣΩΜΑ
ΛΑΒΟΤΣΑ ΕΙΣ ΟΤΡΑΝΙΟΝ ΧΡΙΣΤΟΤ
ΒΑΣΙΛΕΙΑΝ ΜΕΤΑ ΤΩΝ
ΑΓΙΩΝ ΑΝΕΛΗΦΘΗ

"The flesh of Julia Evaresta lies here, but her soul, renewed by the Spirit of Christ, and having received an angelical body, has been taken up into the heavenly kingdom of Christ with the saints."

In an epitaph of the very beginning of the fourth century, or even earlier still, an epitaph to the memory of a Bishop in Calabria begins with the mention of all three Persons of the Blessed Trinity. — The Holy Trinity.

IN D. D. ET SPIRITO SANTO, JULIANO EPP.   *Bull.*, 1873. p. 129; 1876, p. 92.

i.e., "in God, the Lord," (which is, of course, the special title of

[1] See Nos. 1, 7, and 10 in p. 80.

Epitaphs of the Catacombs.

I.C., No. 523. Christ), "and the Holy Spirit." In another the Holy Trinity is spoken of under this very name; but this is a century later, A.D. 403. Unfortunately the stone is broken, so that the epitaph is incomplete. We only know that it was set up to the memory of one Quinctilian, who is called "a man of God," and of whom it is said that he loved chastity and despised the world (*amans castitatem, respuens mundum*); and the line before this begins with the words *confirmans Trinitatem*, whatever those words may mean.

Peculiar phrases with reference to the Holy Trinity.

Marangoni thought that he had discovered in 1742 an heretical formula with reference to the Blessed Trinity in the Cemetery of St. Callixtus. The formula was inscribed on a figure of our Lord, who was represented in the mosaic vaulting of an arcosolium, sitting on a globe as Lord of the world, with St. Peter and St. Paul on either side; and it ran in this wise—*Qui et Filius diceris et Pater inveniris*. To say of our Blessed Lord that, though called the Son, He is found in fact to be no other than the Father, is of course a distinctly heretical proposition; but the inscription does not come from the Cemetery of Callixtus, the real site of which was not at that time known, but from a cemetery of Sabellian heretics into which Marangoni had un-

Bull. 1866, p. 86. wittingly penetrated near Tor Marancia. Another inscription found in a cemetery on the Via Latina might perhaps be suspected of favouring the same heresy. It is, of course, possible to explain the words *Deo Sanc ☧ Uni* in an orthodox sense, but it is not the ordinary language of Christian epigraphy, and it reminds us of an epitaph already referred to, *Qui unu Deu credidit*. Perhaps it is worth observing that on this last-named epitaph the words *in pace* are repeated three times in a most unusual way, as though the writer had been especially anxious to insist upon the orthodoxy of the deceased, and to assert that he had died in the communion of the Church. If these inscriptions had been of earlier date, we should have been disposed to suspect some secret reference to the Sabellian controversy in the days of St. Callixtus, and that they belonged to men who had taken a prominent part in vindicating at that time the doctrine of the monarchy of the First Person of the Holy Trinity. More probably, however, they are of the fourth century, and refer to some later phase of the controversy.

An inscription found in the Cemetery of St. Callixtus in 1865 *Bull.*, 1865, p. 11. uses a term to express the object of Christian worship which entitles it to special mention in this place. The first two lines of the inscription only record that it was set up by a husband to the memory of his wife (*Birginiæ suæ*), and then it continues :—

    QUOD SUMMITAS DEDIT ASIGNABIT
    BENEMERENTI IN PACE

The interpretation of these words is not easy, especially as from the interchange of the letters B and V in *Birginiæ* one cannot be sure whether the verb should be read in the future tense or in the perfect. In the former case, perhaps it should be interpreted as an expression of faith in the resurrection, that God will restore to her at some future day the life which He had given her ; in the latter, the meaning is more obvious ; it becomes an acknowledgment of the Divine decrees and of resignation to them ; that the length of life given to his wife was

Epitaphs of the Catacombs.

assigned to her by God. But in either case, *Summitas* seems clearly to be used here for God; and De Rossi quotes in illustration of it a sentence of Arnobius, who (he says) lived about the same time as this inscription was written, and who speaks of God as having in Himself the height of all perfections (*summitatem omnium summorum obtinens*).[1]

This will be the most suitable place also in which to introduce another epitaph, differing in many respects from the general type of those we have seen. It was found in the Cemetery of St. Callixtus, near the crypt in which St. Cecilia was buried, and marked the grave of some members of a noble family that was probably connected with her own. Hence the conjectural supplement to the mutilated third name. De Rossi considers it certain that it belongs to the beginning of the third century, though it has some characteristics of an earlier period.

R.S., ii. 116; xxxv. 2.

ΦΡΟΝΤΩΝ
ϹΕΠΤΙΜΙΟϹ ΠΡΑιτεξτΑΤΟs κΑΙΚιλιανόs ?
Ο ΔΟΤΛΟϹ ΤΟΤ θεοΤ ΑΞΙΩϹ ΒΙώσας
ΟΤ ΜΕΤΕΝΟΗϹΑ ΚΑΝ ΩΔΕ ϹΟΙ ΤΠΕΡϹΤΗϹΑ
ΚΑΙ ΕΤΚΑριστΗϹΩ ΤΩ ΟΝΟΜΑΤΙ ϹΟΤ ΠΑρέδωκε
ΤΗΝ ΨΤΚψν τΩ ΘΕΩ ΤΡΙΑΝΤΑ ΤΡΙΩν ἐτῶν
ΕΞ ΜΗΝΩΝ

"Septimius Prætextatus Cæcilianus, servant of God, who has led a worthy life. If I have served Thee [O Lord], I have not repented, and I will give thanks to Thy name. He gave up his soul to God (at the age of) thirty-three years and six months."

It is not worth while to point out the errors of orthography in this inscription; but the reader will observe the confusion of persons (which is not uncommon in these monuments), the first and last portions being spoken of the deceased by his surviving friend Fronto, who either wrote or carved the inscription, and the intermediate portion being put into the mouth of the deceased himself.

---

[1] Disput. adv. Gentes., lib. 1.

Dogmatic Allusions.

Next after God, it follows naturally to speak of the angels. But there is hardly any mention of these in ancient Christian epigraphy. Once they appear in their proper character as God's messengers, the dead being said to have been "fetched by the angels;" and once they are named in some other relation, which, however, the mutilated condition of the tablet—one of those which have been already quoted, to the memory of one who "believed in God and in Christ"—unfortunately prevents us from recognising.

The angels.

R.S., ii. xliii. 39.

To the martyrs there is (as might have been expected) far more frequent reference. The title itself was inscribed on the tombs of some of those to whom it belonged, not only in the later and honorary inscriptions by Pope Damasus, but also on the original and contemporary tombstones.

The martyrs.

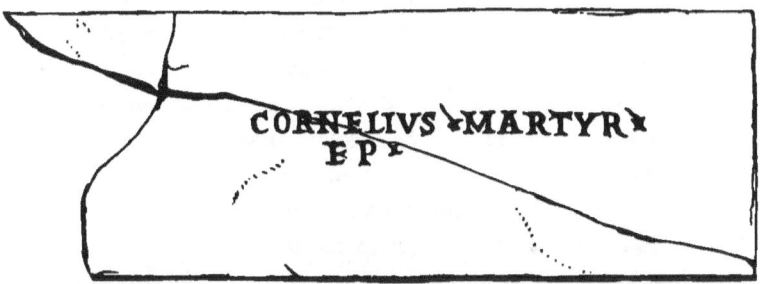

On the tombstone of his predecessor, St. Fabian, the title would seem to have been added after the stone had been fixed in its place, and therefore it is not cut nearly so deep as the other parts of the inscription.

Probably it was necessary to wait for the sanction of the highest authority before it was allowable to give this title to a man;

and after the death of Fabian, the Holy See had remained vacant for eighteen months. The title is found also on another inscription, taken in the year 1845 from the Catacomb of St. Hermes.

DP. III IDUS SEPTEBR YACINTHUS MARTYR

Burial near them much desired.   In the third and fourth centuries the Christians were eager to be buried as near as possible to the tombs of the martyrs, and this desire was prompted by the hope that they would thereby gain an additional interest in their prayers.

ΚΑΤΕΘΑΙΜΗΝ ΕΣ ΤΟ ΑΓΕΙΟΝ ΜΑΡΤΤΡΙ(Ο)Ν

"I buried him at the holy confession (or tomb of the martyrs)."

Parentibus suis tabulam posuit ad sancta martura," "She set up the monument to her parents near the holy martyr [St. Agnes]" is the record of one who had buried them in the cemetery of that saint. *Retro sanctos, ad sanctum Cornelium, ad Ippolitum, ad dominum Gaium, ad sanctam Felicitatem,* are more detailed expressions of the same kind which occur on several epitaphs in the Catacombs; and the theological sense and justification of the practice may be read in the famous treatise of St. Augustine, "*De curâ pro mortuis gerendâ.*"

Martyrs invoked.   Sometimes a direct appeal to the martyr was added on the inscription, asking for his or her protection for the deceased; as in an epitaph from the Catacombs now in the Museum at Naples, which ends with a prayer that St. Laurence will receive

I.R.N., 6736.   the departed soul SANCTE LAURENTI, SUSCEPTA(m h)ABETO ANIMA(m ejus). Another from the same source, now in the private museum of the Marchese del Bagno at Cusercoli, has been already quoted (in pages 25 and 90), in which all the

L.M., ix. 32.   saints are called upon in similar language.

In the Cemetery of St. Hippolytus, Bosio read REFRIGERI TIBI DOMNUS IPOLITUS, just as we may read to-day in the mortar round a grave near the tomb of St. Januarius in the Catacomb of Prætextatus, REFRIGERI JANUARIUS AGATOPUS FELICISSIM MARTYRES. In the Cemetery of Basilla, also known

Dogmatic Allusions. 107

by the name of St. Hermes, on the old Via Salaria, Bosio found the fragment of an inscription on marble, in which a man named Serenus calls upon God ET BEATA BASILLA UT VOBIS, &c. Other epitaphs have been found in the same cemetery during the last century, and may now be seen among the inscriptions in the Lateran Museum, and in our own selection from them (Nos. 4 and 5), in one of which the parents recommend their daughter Crescentina to St. Basilla, and in the other a mother recommends her son to the same powerful protection.

viii. 16, 17.

If the day of death or burial happened to coincide with the martyr's festival, this too was urged as a plea, or recorded as a pledge of special favour and protection. We find this sentiment openly expressed in an old Christian inscription in France, now preserved in the Museum at Carpentras, wherein a widow claims for her husband the intercession of St. Baudelius, the famous martyr of Nîmes, *per passionis die(m)*; *i.e.*, because he had died either on the day of that saint's martyrdom or (unless the Martyrologies are in error) the day following. Her husband had died XII. KAL JUNIAS. SED MARTYR BAUDELIUS PER PASSIONIS DIE DNO DULCEM SUUM COMMENDAT ALUMNUM. In the epitaphs of the Catacombs there are a few chronological notices of the same kind, which, though not so explicit, yet can only be understood in the same sense :—

Their festivals noted.

L.B., ii. 596.

    PECORI DULCIS ANIMA BENIT IN CIMITERO VII. IDUS
    JUL. DP. POSTERA DIE MARTURORUM.

L.M., viii. 25.

"Pecoris, a sweet soul, came into the cemetery on the 9th of July; buried the next day to the Feast of the Martyrs,"

i.e., of the seven sons of Felicitas, who were thus spoken of in Rome as the martyrs *par excellence*.

    ANTE NATALE DOMNI ASTERI(i) DEPOSITUS IN PACE
    "Before the Feast of St. Asterius, buried in peace."
    IN NATALE DOMNES SITIRETIS TERTIUM IDUS FEBB.
    "On the 11th of February, the Feast of St. Soteris (A.D. 401)."

I.C., p. 212.

As the holy confessors and martyrs were allowed during life to plead their own sufferings in mitigation of some portion of the canonical penance inflicted by the discipline of those days upon others who had fallen away in time of persecution, so it was only natural that, as the anniversary of their passion came round, an appeal should be made to them in heaven to use their powers of intercession on behalf of their *alumni*, just now gone to judgment. For this was the relation in which the faithful considered themselves to stand towards the martyrs whom they invoked, as clients towards patrons. "Farewell, dearest son," are the words which the poet Prudentius puts into the mouth of a mother giving up her son to martyrdom,— "Farewell, and when you have entered into Christ's kingdom, remember your mother, then my patron, though now only my son" (*jam patrone ex filio*).[1] *Sancti Petre Marcelline suscipite vestrum alumnum*, said an epitaph of the fifth century in the cemetery where those saints were buried.

Bull., 1875, p. 29.

It is in this sense that we must understand an inscription from the Catacombs which says of a child who died at the age of ten years, that he had been "brought up for God, Christ, and the martyrs" (*Nutricatus Deo Cristo Marturibus*). Both Prudentius and St. Paulinus of Nola bear testimony to the practice to which this inscription seems to refer, viz., of vowing or consecrating children from their tenderest age to the service of God at the shrines of the martyrs. Ancient medals also have been found representing the ceremony of this consecration at the shrine of St. Laurence. An epitaph from Ostia placed in Column I. of the Lateran collection, and belonging either to Anicius Auchenius Bassus, who was Consul A.D. 408, or to his son, who filled the same office twenty years later, and to his wife and family, says of them all that they were *Deo sanctisque devoti;* and the inscriptions on offerings made to various altars or churches about the same date ran in the same form —*De donis Dei et Sanctorum ; de donis Dei et Sanctæ Mariæ, S. Petri,* &c. De Rossi calls attention to the unguarded simplicity of this language, as though those who used it were at no

L.M., viii. 14.

R.S., ii. 302.

Bull., 1869, p. 33.

---

[1] Prudent. Peristeph., x. 813.

pains to express any distinction between God and the saints, because it was known to everybody, and there was no possible danger of scandal through any suspicion that it had been lost sight of. In mediæval and modern times men would not have dared to use the same concise language; from the year 1000 the approved mode of expressing the same truth would have been rather in this form: *Deo ad honorem sanctorum martyrum.* Perhaps some such distinction is virtually expressed in an epitaph to be seen in the column we are still engaged with, wherein it is said of one Mandrosa that she was faithful (or a believer) in Christ, keeping His commandments, *et martyrum obsequiis devota.* viii. 20.

The martyrs were thus honoured and revered as the special friends of God; and men had confidence in the efficacy of their prayers, because they knew that they were now in His presence, and enjoying a participation in His own everlasting life; as we read in another of these epitaphs, which, however, did not belong to a martyr, but only to one of the faithful :—

GENTIANUS FIDELIS IN PACE QUI VIX viii. 15.
IT ANNIS XXI. MENSS VIII. DIES
XVI. ET IN ORATIONIS TUIS
ROGES PRO NOBIS QUIA SCIMUS TE IN ☧

"Gentianus, one of the faithful, in peace, who lived twenty-one years eight months and sixteen days. And in your prayers pray for us, because we know you [to be] in Christ."

CHAPTER VII.

THEIR TESTIMONY TO CERTAIN POINTS OF DISCIPLINE AND PRACTICE.

Evidence from the inscriptions of the Catacombs to—(1) *The hierarchy, pope, bishop, priest, deacon, exorcist, lector, fossor, or ostiarius*—(2.) *Widows and virgins*—(3.) *The laity, fideles, fratres, neophytes, catechumens*—(4.) *The sacraments of baptism, confirmation, and Holy Eucharist.*

Testimony from the Catacombs to other subjects.

IN the present chapter we propose to mention a few other subjects, connected more or less closely with Christian doctrine, upon which some light may be thrown by a careful examination of the inscriptions from the Catacombs; such as the hierarchy of the Church, the different ranks or classes, both of its clergy and laity; its sacraments, and perhaps some minor points of doctrine or discipline.

(1.) The hierarchy.

Bull., 1864, p. 50.

Of the hierarchy, we could almost reconstruct its several degrees from the monuments of ancient Christianity which still remain in the Catacombs. Originally, indeed, it seems probable that even bishops were buried without any title of their office being added to the name engraved on the tombstone; at least if De Rossi and others are correct in referring to the successor of St. Peter a sarcophagus which was found near the "Confession" of that Apostle early in the seventeenth century, with the name LINUS upon it, and nothing more.

Anyhow, it is certain that the terminology by which the different orders were distinguished was not from the beginning solemnly and irrevocably determined. The word *episcopus*, for example, had been in use among the Greeks, sometimes as the title of a commissioner appointed to regulate the affairs of a

Points of Discipline and Practice. 111

new colony, sometimes for the president of the public games and athletic sports, sometimes also for the *magister* of the clubs or *sodalitia* which were so numerous amongst them.[1] Nevertheless it is certain that this word was in common use among Christians as a recognised ecclesiastical title long before the practice of burial in the Catacombs was discontinued. Thus the contracted forms, ΕΠΙ, ΕΠΙΟ, or ΕΡ, have been found upon the tombstones of Anteros, Fabian, Eutychianus, and Cornelius, all bishops of Rome during the third century. We have seen that of Cornelius in p. 105, and facsimiles of the others are given in the next page.

<small>Bishops.</small>

Even the title of *papa* was used as an ecclesiastical title before the end of the fourth century.

<small>Pope.</small>

A fragment of an inscription which came to light in 1876 in the course of the excavations for the modern cemetery at San Lorenzo *fuori le mura* consists of these letters :—

<small>*Bull.*, 1876, p. 17.</small>

RA
A CUMPAVIT
ONUS SE BIBO
E PAPA LIBERIO

The first two lines tell us of some deacon or some person whose name ended in *onus* having bought a grave for himself, and the engraver having made a blunder in one of his words, supplied the omission by inserting the two letters in smaller type above the line. The interest of the inscription is centred, of course, in the mention of Pope Liberius in the last line, and the question is, What word is to be supplied before *papa*? It must be some word in the ablative case ending in *e*, and De Rossi says that, according to the analogy of other tombstones, only two can be suggested, *concedente* or *sedente*. In support of the former there might be quoted from his own volume of dated inscriptions a grave *concessus a Papa Hormisda*, and another *concessus a beatissimo Papa Joanne*. But these belong to the sixth century and to the Vatican Basilica. In an earlier

[1] See Aristoph., Aves, 1022; O. II., 4024; Spon, Misc. Antiq., xx. 3.

ANTEPWC ETTI

ΦABIANOC ETTI f M

ΛΟΥΚΙС

ΕΥΤΥΧΙΑΝΟС ΕΠΙС

age we have only evidence of the Pope exercising immediate jurisdiction over the Cemetery of St. Callixtus, and even at the time when Popes Hormisdas and John were granting places of burial in the Vatican, we have proof that a similar privilege was conceded at San Lorenzo, not by the Pope, but by the Provost of the church, *Præpositus*. Moreover, the present inscription does not record a gratuitous concession, but a purchase. De Rossi concludes, therefore, that the missing word must have been *sedente*, and he continues as follows:—"Amid so many thousands of Christian sepulchral inscriptions in Rome belonging to the first six centuries, I only knew of two examples up to the present day in which the name of the Pope was made thus to take the place of the Consul's. I say in sepulchral inscriptions, because in sacred or historical inscriptions in basilicas, and every kind of votive and religious dedication, *salvo episcopo* was the accustomed and legitimate formula" (corresponding to the Pagan chronological formula, *Salvis Augustis nostris*). "Now of the two examples, one belonged to Damasus, SUB DAMASO EPISCO, and the other was precisely Liberius. This last, however, was found in a mutilated condition, SUB LIBE, and the example of the other inscription suggested to me to supply SUB LIBERIO EPISCOPO. And I went on to make this further remark, that both of the Roman Pontiffs whose names had been thus singularly used had had to contend with schism. The election of Damasus had been disturbed by the competition of Ursicinus; and when Liberius was exiled for the faith, Constantius tried to make the much controverted Felix first his substitute, and then his colleague. The Roman people, however, cried out with loud shouts, 'One God, one Christ, one bishop,'[1] and remained faithful to Liberius. Hence the singular formulæ under discussion are not to be taken as chronological dates so much as protestations of obedience to the legitimate pastor of the Church. And now to-day we find a third monument, containing another formula

[1] Theodoret, Hist. Eccl., ii. 17.

of the same kind with reference to Liberius, and its peculiarity confirms the view I have taken, that it has reference not to the mere fact of Liberius's pontificate generically, but to the tempestuous circumstances of the time under which both the Roman Senate and people, remaining faithful to Liberius, protested against the intrusion of Felix, and rising up, drove him out of the city.[1] This devotion of the Catholic flock to Liberius, returned from exile, is a point of considerable historical importance; it is a strong argument in his favour in the controversy which has been so warmly agitated as to his constancy in the faith for which he was persecuted and banished. All monuments, therefore, which allude to this devotion and obedience of the people have a notable value, and should be carefully weighed by those who make a special study of the controversies of ecclesiastical history."

But this monument has yet another value. The word *pope* is employed here absolutely as expressive of an office or dignity; it is not an expression of mere filial affection on the part of the flock towards their shepherd, as it is when we find it used with the addition of a personal pronoun, " our pope," or " his pope " —*e.g.*, in an epitaph (quoted in page 46) of the end of the third century, a deacon says that he had made a chamber in the Catacombs with the consent of his Pope Marcellinus (*jussu Papæ sui Marcellini*). Here *papa* is used in its old and ordinary sense as patron or father, as it is used also in some of the Acts of the Martyrs—*e.g.*, St. Perpetua says to the Bishop Optatus, " You are our *papa;*" and on another occasion the Pagan judges begin their examination of a priest who is brought before them with this question, " You are Antony, whom they call their *papa*."[2] But here the title is given to Liberius, and in an epitaph of Furius Dionysius Filocalus, found in the Cemetery of St. Callixtus, it is given to his successor Damasus, without

R.S., ii., p. 230.

Bull., 1873, p. 160

---

[1] Marcellini et Faustini, Libellus Precum, Præf., Sismondi, Opp., t. i.
[2] Ruinart, Acta Sincera, ed. Paris, p. 92; Mabillon, Analecta, t. iv. p. 104.

Points of Discipline and Practice. 115

the addition of any qualifying adjective.[1] The Roman clergy wrote of St. Cyprian [2] as *benedictum papam Cyprianum*, and we know from the letters of St. Augustin and St. Jerome, and the poems of Prudentius,[3] that the title was common to all bishops; but Sismondi has shown that, at least from the fifth century, it was given in a special manner to the Bishops of Rome; and the monuments we have now seen prove that this practice had begun at a still earlier period. Not only is Damasus called Pope Damasus on a public monument, but the same title is given to his predecessor even on a common tombstone; and not on one only, for we have recently recovered from the Cemetery of St. Callixtus the missing fragment of the other inscription that has been spoken of, SUB LIBE, and we find that the supplement suggested (*episcopo*) was incorrect; the inscription really ran thus: SUB LIBERIO PAPA. These two notices of "Pope Liberius" from different cemeteries—to which we shall presently add a third from Spoleto—show that the use of the title in an absolute way was familiar to the Christians of Rome from the middle of the fourth century. In like manner, there is evidence that in the East, as early as the days of Arius, there was a tendency to apply the same title to the Bishops of Alexandria in a special way, as distinguished from the bishops of less important sees in the patriarchate. Even in Rome, however, as we learn from paintings still to be seen in the Catacombs, it was not unusual to add ROMANUS after PP, or PAPA, as late as the ninth century.

Pope Damasus himself, when he had occasion in his histori-

---

[1] In the imperfect copy of this well-known monument in the crypt of St. Eusebius—the restoration in the sixth or seventh century of the original by Pope Damasus—we read *Damasis Pappa cultor atque amator*. De Rossi, following the example of the monument of Severus, which speaks of *Papæ sui Marcellini*, supposed that Filocalus had written in the same style, *Damasi Papæ sui*. Subsequently, however, another fragment of the original stone has been recovered, which shows that the *s* was one of the many blunders of the ignorant "restorer"—the fragment gives us *s, i, p* in succession, showing that *papæ* followed the name of Damasus immediately.

[2] Ep. viii., inter Cyprianicas. [3] Peristeph., xi. 127.

116   *Epitaphs of the Catacombs.*

Or Rector.   cal monuments to name any of his predecessors, almost always gave them the title of RECTOR, or ruler. Once in the inscription in the Papal crypt he calls one of them (Melchiades) SACERDOS. He is himself also called RECTOR in an inscription put up to the honour of SS. Felix and Adauctus by a priest named Verus, at his bidding.

L.M., iii. 2.
>   PRESBYTER HIS VERUS, DAMASO RECTORE JUBENTE,
>   COMPOSUIT TITULUM SANCTORUM LIMINA ADORNANS.

Priest.   The few sepulchral fragments which remained in the single area of the crypt of Lucina, when it was rediscovered by De Rossi, gave no less than three memorials of priests, of which the most recent is of a certain Maximus, whom he believes to

R.S.I., xix. 5.   be the celebrated confessor of the year 250. The name of the

most ancient is lost; there only remains the abbreviation ΠP, written in very beautiful letters, and belonging to the oldest part of the cemetery. On the whole, De Rossi does not hesitate to assign it to the second century. Neither is it possible to assign a later date to one which has been recovered from the Cœmeterium Ostrianum, which has all the characteristics of that same ancient and simple style of which we have already seen several specimens in page 33. Like the other examples, it presents us the title of *presbyter*, only in an abbreviated form.

>   AVR. HELIODORVS. P R T.

In the next example the word is given at full length. It is of the first half of the third century, and it appears that the man to whom it was set up (Dionysius) was a physician as well as a priest. Perhaps the same advantages were derived from the

Points of Discipline and Practice. 117

union of these two characters in those days as are experienced in the present day by zealous missionaries of the faith in China and some other heathen countries.

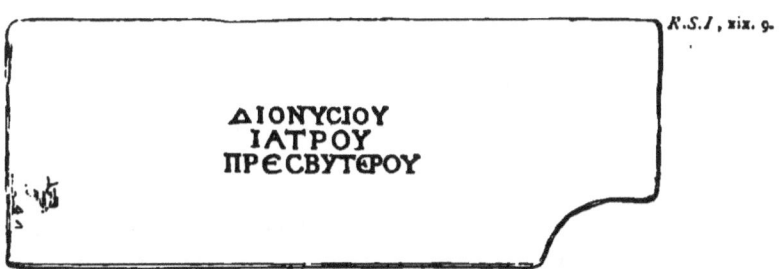

R.S.I, xix. 9.

ΔΙΟΝΥCΙΟΥ
ΙΑΤΡΟΥ
ΠΡЄCΒΥΤЄΡΟΥ

Several other epitaphs of more recent date, yet still very ancient, may be seen in Column X. of the Lateran, in the walls of the staircase by which we descend to the Basilica of St. Agnes, and yet more abundantly in books. *Presbyter* is the word uniformly used, and some of the epitaphs make mention of their wives also as being buried with them—*e.g.*, of the year 389 in the cloisters of St. Paul's, *Gaudentius presb. sibi et conjugi suæ Severæ sanctæ ac sanctissimæ feminæ*, &c.

The deacon Severus also, at the end of the third century, Deacon. would seem to have been married, for he made a double vault in the Cemetery of St. Callixtus, with the leave of "his Pope," Marcellinus, and he says that he made it as a quiet resting-place for himself and those who belonged to him (*sibi suisque*); and then there follows immediately on the same stone the remarkable epitaph which we have already had occasion to quote (page 46), to the memory of a child of ten years old, who was probably his daughter. And there is an epitaph in the xv. 10. Lateran Museum by one Felix a deacon to his wife Aurelia, *Verecundæ, pudicæ, totiusque integritatis fæminæ*. The deacons occupied a very important position in the administrative department of the Church, and especially of the cemeteries, in the second and third centuries. Possibly one of them is designated in an epitaph of the Lateran under the title *Ministrator* x. 20. *Christianus*. A handsome vault in the Cemetery of St. Callixtus would almost seem to have been appropriated for their burial, as the Papal crypt was for the burial of the bishops.

R.S., iii. pp. 236-242.

Of a subdeacon the most ancient monument with which we are acquainted was found in the Cemetery of St. Alexander, about seven miles from Rome, on the Via Nomentana; but it is somewhat too late to allow of its being quoted here, as it belongs to the year 448. And in like manner, of an acolyte, we do not know of any which falls strictly within our limits. The earliest we have seen was once in the pavement of the Church of St. Vitalis, to which title he belonged. He is called *Acol. Reg. Quarte. TT. Vestinæ;* and he was buried on the 8th October (*P*[*ostero*] *D*[*ie*] *Nat. Sti. Marci*), at the age of thirty. Another came to light recently under the pavement of the old Basilica of St. Lorenzo *fuori le mura;* it was inscribed LOCUS ROMANI ACOLITI, and belongs (according to De Rossi) either to the fourth or fifth century. The existence, however, of both these grades of the hierarchy during the period with which we are concerned is attested by a letter addressed to St. Cyprian by those who were condemned to the mines, who write to thank him for his ministrations to the relief of their temporal necessities, which (they say) he had sent to be distributed "by Herennianus the subdeacon (*hypodiaconus*), and Lucianus, Maximus, and Amantius, acolytes."[1] There is also the letter of Pope Cornelius (A.D. 250) to the Bishop of Antioch, in which he enumerates the staff of clergy in Rome as containing "forty-six priests, seven deacons, seven subdeacons, forty-two acolytes, and exorcists, lectors, and *ostiarii*, taken all together, fifty-two."[2]

Subdeacon.

I.C., No. 743.

Acolyte.

Bull., 1863, p. 16.

De Rossi considers it certain that there must be some error with reference to this last numeral. We can easily understand the paucity of the deacons and subdeacons; neither should we have been surprised at finding only a small number of exorcists; but he thinks that there must have been at least as many lectors

R.S., iii. p. 536.

---

[1] Ep. lxxvii.
[2] Euseb. H. E., vi. 43. See Epist. Rom. Pont. ed. Coustant, p. 149.

Points of Discipline and Practice. 119

as acolytes, since their duties obliged them to assist at the solemn reunions of the faithful for the divine offices; neither can there have been fewer doorkeepers than there were *tituli* or parishes, and there were certainly twenty-five at this time. On the whole, therefore, he believes that a numeral must have been dropped out of the text, and that we ought to read either 152, or even 252.

However, be this as it may, there are many monuments of the other orders, both of lectors and exorcists. On a tombstone still lying in its place on the floor of one of the galleries of St. Callixtus we read PAULUS EXORCISTA DEPOSITUS MARTYRIES—*i.e.*, buried near the martyrs (*ad martyres*); and another from the same source, of the fourth century, has CELERI EXORC. CUM COMPARE SUA IN PACE. A third stone, from a catacomb on the other side of Rome, now preserved in the Lateran, exhibits PRIMUS EXORCISTA FECIT. And we must make room for yet another, though it does not belong to Rome, but to the north of Italy; neither are we able to define its age very precisely. Both Mommsen and De Rossi are satisfied as to its authenticity; and the latter author tells us that most modern authors assign it to the fourth century, though their predecessors had thought it was earlier. Flavius Latinus, whose monument it is, was Bishop of Brescia; and the remarkable thing is, that his granddaughter, who set it up, should have thought it worth while to commemorate not only how long he was bishop and priest, but also how long he was exorcist.

Exorcist.
R.S., i. xxxvii.
28.
Bull., 1868, p. 11.

x 13.

C.I.L., v. 4846.

Bull., 1876, p. 91.

FL·LATINO·EPISCOPO·ANN·III·M·VII·PRÆSB
AN·XV·EXORC·AN·XII·ET·LATINILLÆ·ET·FLA
MACRINO·LECTORI·FL·PAULINA·NEPTIS
B·M·M·P.

"To Flavius Latinus, who was bishop for three years seven months; priest for fifteen years; exorcist for twelve years; and to Latinilla, and to Flavius Macrinus, lector; Flavia Paulina, his granddaughter, put this up to his good memory (*bona memoriæ posuit*)."

Of lectors there are both more numerous and more ancient records. One is even found among those most ancient epi-

Lector.

taphs of the Cœmeterium Ostrianum which cannot be put later than the first half of the second century. It consists merely of the name (repeated twice, and corrected as the reader sees), the title, and the primitive symbol of the anchor.

Bull., 1871, p. 32.

FAVOR. FAO̅R (*anchor*) LECTOR

Another, bearing marks of the same primitive antiquity, is now preserved in the ducal palace at Urbino, and marked the tomb of a lector and his wife, CLAUDIUS ATTICIANUS LECTOR ET CLAUDIA FELICISSIMA CO(N)JUX. In later monuments of this class it is generally added to which of the titles, churches, or ecclesiastical divisions of the city they belong. One, *Regionis Secundæ*, is of the year 338; another, *de Pallacine*—*i.e.*, of the church which is now called St. Mark's, A.D. 348; a third, *tituli Fasciolæ*, A.D. 377; and a fourth, *Leopardus Lector de Pudentianâ*—*i.e.*, of the title of St. Pudens (*ecclesia Pudentiana*), A.D. 384. The age of the first of these was only nineteen, of the third forty-six, and of the last twenty-four.

I.C., Nos. 62, 164, and 388.
Bull., 1867, p. 51.

Fossor [or ostiarius].

x. 21-33.

We find no distinct mention of *ostiarii*, or doorkeepers; but it seems extremely probable that their place was filled in those early days by the *fossores*, or diggers of the subterranean cemeteries, of whom there are most abundant memorials. We have seen that the *ostiarii* are mentioned among the classes of persons supported by the Roman Church in the days of Pope Cornelius—*i.e.*, in the middle of the third century—and the *fossores* are not; and yet it is certain that they existed, and that their maintenance must have been provided for by the Church. On the other hand, in some other lists of the Roman clergy, made at a somewhat later period, the *fossores* are enumerated and the *ostiarii* are not. And a moment's reflection will satisfy us that the *fossores* must certainly have fulfilled all the most essential duties of the *ostiarii* as long as the holy mysteries were celebrated during the ages of persecution in the subterranean chambers of the Catacombs.

Points of Discipline and Practice. 121

After enumerating the several grades of the clergy, our thoughts turn naturally to consecrated members of the other sex, virgins and widows—that is to say, women who from motives of religion abstained from marriage altogether, or at least from contracting it twice. Of both of these, distinct mention is made in the Epistles of St. Paul. The earliest Christian apologists too are unanimous in extolling the love of the faithful for the state of virginity and the continence of widows, so that it would have been strange if the ancient Christian epitaphs should not have borne some testimony to them. *(1.) Widows and virgins.* *1 Cor. vii.; 1 Tim. v.*

First, we observe that the word *virgo* is often recorded in them, even where, from the age of the deceased, it would have seemed quite unnecessary. In estimating its significance, however, we must bear in mind the very early age at which Roman girls were married. Twelve was the age determined by law, and several inscriptions, both Pagan and Christian, testify that this age was far from being unknown in practice. *Virgins.* *Gruter. pp. 751, 752, 813–815; O.H., 2742.*

Hence the following inscriptions are not so unmeaning as they may at first sight appear. The first is of the year 295: STATILIA ALEXANDRA ANNORUM XIIII VIRGO MORTUA EST. Another runs thus:—

BACCIS DULCIS ANIMA	PATER	*R.S.*, iii. xxx. 47.
IN PACAE DOMINI QUÆ	FILIÆ SU(Æ)	
VIXI(T) ANNOS XV. VIRGO	DULCISSIMÆ	
DIES LXX. PRIDIE CALENDAS DECE(M)BRES.		

"Baccis, sweet soul, in the peace of the Lord; who lived fifteen years and seventy days, a virgin. November 30th. Her father, to his sweetest daughter."

Another belongs to the year 401: PRETIOSA ANNORUM XII. TANTUM ANCILLA DEI ET CHRISTI. It is disputed whether any special dedication to religion is to be understood by this title of "Handmaid of God and of Christ." At first sight we should have been disposed to think that some such meaning was tolerably certain; on the other hand, we find Tertullian, in the opening of his second book on "Female Dress," address- *R.S., i. xxv. 2.* *Ancilla Dei et Christi.*

ing those to whom he writes as "handmaids of the living God, my fellow-slaves (of Christ) and sisters;"[1] and yet it is clear that that work was not written for the use only of those whom we now call "religious." There can be less doubt, however, about the religious character of a lady aged twenty-eight, who is called "a virgin of God" on her epitaph, now to be seen in the Kircherian Museum: VICTORA BIRGO DEI QUI VIXIT ANNIS XXVIIL IN PACE III. IDUS FEBR. It is worthy of remark that the title *Famulus Dei*, or servant of God, for which Scriptural authority might be quoted,[2] and which is so common on the ancient inscriptions of Spain, does not often occur on the early Christian epitaphs of Rome. We have seen it once (in Greek) in our last chapter, but we hardly know another instance before the fifth century. The phrase *Homo Dei*, which probably was intended to mean much the same thing, is met with more than once in the Catacombs.

Famulus Dei. L.B.I. 124.

Homo Dei.

But to return to the title of virgin. It is given to a stranger (*peregrina*), aged forty-one years, in No. 17 of our selection; also, in No. 21, to a man aged twenty-three, of whom his parents record that he went out of this world "a virgin and a neophyte." De Rossi has met with another example in the Cemetery of St. Callixtus, where the title is given to a man:—

R.S., ii. xlvii. 51.

PONTIUS ATENAGORAS QUI VIX. AN. XXII. VIRGO.

In the column at the Lateran, from which most of our specimens are taken, there are other examples of neophyte virgins—*e.g.*, Nos. 27 and 28; and the first of these had only just completed her ninth year. Indeed, those who are called virgins are of very various ages. No. 1 is a lady aged thirty-five, "more or less;" No. 5, "a virgin, a girl of seventeen;" No. 6, "a faithful virgin," of the same age.

---

[1] See also De Uxore, ii. 6; but in De Virg. Vel., c. 3, we have *Christi solius ancillæ* spoken of virgins.
[2] Rom. i. 1; Acts xvi. 17.

Points of Discipline and Practice. 123

At No. 7 we find a man named Parthenius, whose name *Virginius or Virginia.* reminds us of the Latin version of the same name continually given on Christian epitaphs both to husbands and wives —Virginius or Virginia. It may even be found on a few Pagan epitaphs. It refers, of course, to their condition before marriage, and means that they had never been married before.

An inscription of the year 291 runs in this wise:—

> EX VIRGINIO TUO BEN *I.C.,* i. p. 23.
> E MECO VIXSISTI LIB ENIC
> ONJUGA INNOCENTISSI
> MA CERVONIA SILVANA
> REFRIGERA CUM SPIRITA
> SANCTA DEP KAL APR TIBERI
> ANO II ET DIONI COSS.

Perhaps the three first words of this inscription ought to be taken separately from what follows, and be understood as merely stating who set up this memorial; "from your husband." Or they may be taken as intended to be equivalent to the Scriptural account of the Prophetess Anna, "who had lived with her husband seven years from her virginity;" and we may translate as follows:—

"Cervonia Silvana, most innocent wife, thou hast lived well and willingly (*libenter?*) with me, thy husband, from thy virginity. Be refreshed with the holy souls. Buried on the 1st of April, A.D. 291."

The high esteem in which chastity and continence were held in the Christian community is attested in another way by an epithet sometimes attached to the name of a wife on her tombstone, μόνανδρος, Univira, or Unibyra.

> CEMΠPONIA ΓTNH CEMNH MONANΔPOC. *Univira.*
>
> "Sempronia, venerable lady, who never had but one husband." *R.S.,*iii. xxii. 17.

The same feeling dictated the following at the end of an epitaph

<small>xvii. 13.</small> in the Catacombs, now to be seen in the Lateran: TE IN PACE CUM VIRGINITATE TUA. The girl to whom this apostrophe is addressed was between fifteen and sixteen. Another epitaph, from the Cemetery of St. Callixtus, if we are to understand it strictly, goes a great deal further than this, for it affirms of a lady that she led a life of perfect continence, even in the <small>R.S., i. xxx. 13.</small> married state, for five years: VIXIT INLIBATA CUM VIRGINIO SUO ANNOS V.

Widows.   Of the epitaphs of widows, the Lateran Museum contains two or three examples. In the first, the matron (Octavia) is <small>xi. 2.</small> called *Vidua Dei;* where the title "widow of God" must certainly mean some special consecration to the service of God in the condition of widowhood. St. Paul speaks of <small>1 Tim. v. 9. 16.</small> widows being "chosen," who were not less than threescore years of age, and who had not been married to more than one husband. If they had any relatives among the faithful, such relatives were bound to minister to their wants, "that the Church might not be charged (*gravetur*), and there may be sufficient for them that are widows indeed." And the reader will see in our selection (No. 19) the epitaph of one Daphne, a widow, who "as long as she lived never charged the Church" .(*cum vixit, ecclesiam nihil gravavit*). A third epitaph, from the Catacomb of St. Saturninus, bears precisely the same testimony to another widow. The monument is put up by her daughter, who says that she had been the wife of one husband, that she "sat" a widow for sixty years, and lived to be upwards of eighty. The word "sat" has an official sound about it, but it was probably only meant to say that Regina had lived in the state of widowhood for that number of years, since we are expressly told that she never burdened the Church; and even if her circumstances had been different, she would not have been eligible, according to the rules of discipline laid down by St. Paul, until she was threescore years of age.

```
REGINE VENEMERENTI FILIA SUA FECIT
VENE REGINE MATRI VIDUA QUE SE
DIT VIDUA ANNOS LX ET ECLESA
NUNQUA GRAVAVIT UNIBYRAQUE
VIXIT ANNOS LXXX MESIS V.
DIES XXVI.[1]
```

"To the well-deserving Regina. Her daughter made this to her well-deserving mother, Regina, who sat a widow sixty years, and never burdened the Church, and never had but one husband. She lived eighty years five months and twenty-six days."

After these privileged classes, it follows to speak of the great body of the faithful. This was their proper title, πιστοί or *fideles*. This is the word used both in Holy Scripture and in these ancient epitaphs. It was a title to which a man had no claim until he had been baptized. By that sacrament we receive the gift of faith, as the first question in the form of administering it still sufficiently indicates—"What dost thou seek from the Church of God?—Faith." Hence in these short inscriptions, and in other documents also of the same antiquity—*e.g.*, the letter of Pope Cornelius, quoted in an earlier part of this chapter—baptism is sometimes spoken of under the phrases *fidem accepit*, or *percepit*, or absolutely (the noun being understood) *percepit, consecuta est*. Or *fides* is put absolutely for baptism, as when Tertullian says that it is not allowed to contract a second marriage *post fidem*, or speaks of those who have fallen into grievous sin after baptism as *post fidem lapsi*.[2] In a monument of the year 268 the same truth is expressed in another form, "*gratiam accepit D.N.*," "received the grace of our Lord;" and the same also occurs in a Greek inscription. In another, a man is said to be *fide constitutus*, and the day of baptism is called the day of *acceptio* or *consecutio*.

(3.) The Laity.

The Faithful.
1 Tim. v. 16.
L.M., xi. 8-11.

Bull., 1869, p. 27.

I.C., No. 10, p. 16.

```
PERIT ANN. XXXV.
EX DIE ACCEPTIONES SUÆ VIXIT DIES LVII.
```

"She died at the age of thirty-five. From the day of her receipt (of baptism) she lived fifty-seven days."

---

[1] Marchi, *Monumenti delle Arti Cristiane Primitive*, p. 98.
[2] De Pudic., cc., 1 and 18.

CONSECUTUS EST IIL NON. DECEMB. EX DIE CONSECVTIONIS
IN SÆCULO FUIT AD USQUE VII. IDUS DECEMB.

"He received [baptism] on the 3d of December, and from the day of his attainment of it, he remained in the world till the 7th of December."

The last inscription is taken from a Christian cemetery in Africa, not in Rome; but it was worth quoting for its exact conformity with the one which precedes it. In both alike there is the same distinction between the natural and the spiritual age of the deceased—*i.e.*, between his first and his second birth. After stating the number of years he had lived in the world, his age is computed afresh from the day of his regeneration, thus marking off the length of his spiritual from that of his merely natural life; as Tertullian tells us was the common habit of Christians; "our very life," he says, "is counted only from our baptism (*a fide etiam ipsa vita nostra censetur;*"[1] and the biographer of St. Cyprian in like manner says that "the deeds of the man of God ought not to be reckoned except from the date of his birth to God."

A very interesting Roman inscription tells us of a child not yet two years old, who was tenderly loved by his grandmother, and when she saw that he was taken for death, she begged from the Church that he should go out of this world as one of the faithful (*cum soldu* [solide] *amatus fuisset a majore sua et vidit hunc morti consti*[*tu*] *tum esse petivit de æclesia ut fidelis de seculo recessisset*). In an inscription of the year 382 we have the record of one of the "faithful," aged sixteen months. And here is another very much older, having about it, indeed, every mark of special antiquity, both in its language and its symbols (the fish and the anchor), which records the death of a child between two and three years old, who is stated to have been both one of the faithful himself and born of faithful parents.

[1] De Monog., c. xi.

Points of Discipline and Practice.

ΠΙCTOC ΕΚ ΠΙC
ΤΩΝ ΖΩCIMOC
ΕΝΘΑΔΕ ΚΕΙΜΕ
ΖΗCΑC · ΕΤΕCΙΝ
Β · ΜΗ · Α ΗΜΕ ΚΕ

L.M., xiv. 19.

"I lie here, Zosimus, faithful, and (born) of faithful (parents), having lived two years one month and twenty-five days."

In a long and curious inscription preserved in the Museum of the Louvre in Paris, a child (*infans dulcissima atque inno-* *Bull.*,1868,p.75. *centissima*) is said to have been "born a Pagan on the 6th of March, and after eighteen months and twenty-two days complete, to have been made one of the faithful (*fidelis facta*) at eight o'clock in the evening, and to have died four hours afterwards. She died at one o'clock in the morning, on the 25th of September." This inscription does not belong to our sub- *I.C.*, i. xi. ject geographically, for it came from the Christian cemetery of Catania in Sicily, but it may very properly be used by way of illustration, since it falls within our chronological limits as a monument of the fourth century.

Another title by which the faithful were habitually known *Fratres.* to one another, and (there is good reason to believe) to others also, was *fratres*, or brethren. It was hardly to be expected that this title should occur on the sepulchral inscriptions of the Catacombs, since it belonged to the whole community, and would be used only when there was occasion to speak of them in their collective capacity, whereas each individual would be described according to his position in the Church; according to his ecclesiastical office, if he held any, or according to his relation to the sacraments and communion of the Church, if he were a layman—*e.g.*, a catechumen, if he had died whilst under instruction, and before he had been admitted into the fold by baptism; a neophyte, if he died soon after receiving that holy sacrament; *fidelis*, if the white robes of his baptism had been laid aside, and he had lived and died in the enjoyment of all the rights and privileges of a Christian. Hence this last is the most common designation on the epitaphs; a few monuments, however, of the early ages still remain on which the title of *fratres* occurs. We have seen one such already (p. 95), in which an appeal is made to the brethren to pray for a deceased lady. In the following, found by De Rossi in the Catacomb of St. Priscilla, and referred by him to an early part of the third century, "the brethren" ask peace from God for the deceased Leontius, LEONTI PAX A FRATRIBUS VALE; and on a third, from the Catacomb of St. Cyriaca, Boldetti read ULPIA VIVA SIS CUM FRATRIBUS TUIS ("Ulpia, mayest thou live with thy brethren"). We find in Greek at the end of an epitaph set up by a father and mother to their son, "who had well received the grace of God," ΕΙΡΗΝΗΝ ΕΧΕΤΕ ΑΔΕΛΦΟΙ, which we may almost render "Peace be with you, brethren."

<small>Bull.,1864, p. 12.</small>

<small>1869, p. 27.</small>

Public monuments on which this title was used have been discovered in various places. One was dug up in the ruins of an old Roman town not far from Algiers, and records the grant of an area for a Christian cemetery and the erection of a small church. The donor salutes "the brethren," "born of the Holy Spirit with a pure and simple heart." In another monument found at the same spot the priest Victor states that "he made this place for all the brethren." At Cumenia in Phrygia, a pillar has been found bearing on one side an inscription to the memory of five sons who "at one and the same time purchased for themselves a share in life "—*i.e.*, in eternal life, probably by martyrdom; and on the other side, "All on the eastern side up to this point is common to the brethren" —ΕΙΣ ΤΗΝΔΕ ΤΟ ΗΩΟΝ ΚΟΙΝΟΝ ΤΩΝ ΑΔΕΛΦΩΝ. Others belong to Salone, to Heraclea in Pontus, and to other places; and the agreement of so many monuments in so many different localities seems to warrant the conclusion that this was the official title (so to speak) of the Christian community; that whereas the members of private religious or social bodies (especially of burial-clubs) among Pagans were called *sodales*, Christians were called *fratres*. There was indeed one Pagan

<small>R.S., i. 106.</small>

sodality into whose title this word entered, the *Fratres Arvales*, but this was because the story of their foundation supposed them to have succeeded to twelve real brothers, the sons of Acca Laurentia.[1] Sometimes also the officials of other *collegia* would call their members "brothers" by way of compliment and courtesy, just as the patrons and founders of such institutions were sometimes called Fathers or Mothers. But it was reserved for Christianity to create a real brotherhood among men of different ranks and races. It is only within the fold of the Church that "the rich and poor have really met one another,"[2] having all things common during life, and after death being laid to rest side by side in one common cemetery; or, as Minucius Felix expresses it, "we call ourselves brethren, because we are children of one parent, God; are partakers in one faith, and fellow-heirs of the same hope."

It has been already mentioned that persons newly baptized were called neophytes, *i.e.*, lately born, newly planted in Christ through the initiatory sacrament of His grace. The title occurs in Holy Scripture,[3] and is often inscribed on the epitaphs. We have given two examples (Nos. 20 and 21) in our selection, and many more may be seen in the Lateran. They are also called νεοφώτιστοι, or newly illuminated, because to them were revealed the mysteries of the faith, which were carefully concealed from the mere catechumens. Moreover, by the Sacrament of Baptism they received the grace of God, which imparted a new power, and spread a new light over their souls. "This bath of regeneration," says Justin Martyr,[4] "is called illumination, because those who learn these things have their understandings illuminated." Hence "*illuminare*" is used as equivalent to *baptizare*; and an ancient Christian writer,[5] speaking of the two Sacraments of Baptism and the Holy

Neophyte.

---

[1] Henzen, Atti dei Frat. Arv., p. 1.
[2] Prov. xxii. 2.
[3] 1 Tim. iii. 6.
[4] Apolog., i. 61.
[5] St. Prosper of Aquitania, or the author of the book "De Promiss. et Prædic. Dei," which goes by his name, ii. 39.

130   *Epitaphs of the Catacombs.*

Eucharist, says that we are enlightened by the one and fed by the other. The title νεοφώτιστος may be read on several epitaphs, which, being in Greek, are probably very ancient—*e.g.*,

I. M., xi. 18, 19.
R.S., iii. xxiv. 1;
xxviii. 44.

ΔΙΟΝΤCΙC ΝΕΟΦΩΤΙC ΕΝΙΑΝΤΟΤ ΕΝΟC ΜΗΝΩΝ ΤΕCCΑΡΩΝ.

"Dionysius, newly illuminated. (A child) of one year four months."

Among the dated inscriptions, which (as our readers will remember) begin to multiply towards the latter half of the fourth century, we have instances of the Sacrament of Baptism administered to children of five, six, eight, and nine years, and also to adults of twenty-eight and forty-two. During the first week after baptism, whilst they still retained their white garments, they were called *infantes* and *pueri*; and this title was not confined to those who were really children according to the flesh; for St. Augustin[1] tells us of Victorinus, the famous Roman rhetorician, that "though old, he was not ashamed to be called a child (*puer*) of Christ and an infant of God's font."

Catechumen.
xi. 29

At No. 22 of our selection we give an example of a catechumen, or person under instruction for baptism, aged eight years; the other example in the Lateran is of a Greek, named Andragathos; his age is not specified.

(4.) The Sacraments of Baptism and

Full. 1869. p. 30.

A Greek inscription was found a few years since on the Via Latina, recording of a lady who had belonged to one of the Gnostic sects in the third century, that she had been "anointed in the baths of Christ with His pure and incorruptible ointment"—an inscription which manifestly refers to two separate rites in use among the Gnostics, in imitation of two of the Christian sacraments. In an inscription of the latter part of the fourth century one of these sacraments is expressed by washing, the other by anointing; and St. Cyprian, a hundred and twenty years earlier, had used the same word to denote confirmation. "It is necessary," he says, "that he who has been baptized should be also anointed, that having received the chrism, *i.e.*, the unction, he may become *Unctus Dei.*" The epitaph of a Christian lady buried in Spoleto calls it by

Confirmation.

c.u., 18-1, p.
1.xx., 1860. p. 23.

[1] Confess., viii. 2.

Points of Discipline and Practice. 131

another name; and it records that she was a neophyte, and had been *consignata* by Pope Liberius: this, of course, belongs to the middle of the fourth century. And we read of a boy who died when he was a little more than five years old, *Bimus trimus consecutus est*—words which were a veritable enigma to all antiquarians, until the learned Marini compared with them the phrases of Roman law, *bima trima die dos reddita, bima trima die legatum solutum,* and pointed out that as these phrases undoubtedly signified that such a portion of the dowry or legacy was paid in the second year, and such another portion in the third, so the corresponding words in the Christian epitaph could only mean that the deceased had received something when he was two years old, and something else when he was three; and although the particular gifts received are not mentioned, we can have no difficulty in supplying baptism and confirmation. De Rossi adopts this interpretation; indeed, it does not seem possible to suggest any other.

Moreover, when seeking for evidence in the Catacombs with reference to the Sacrament of Confirmation, we must remember that this was generally administered in olden times immediately after baptism, of which it was considered the complement and perfection. "From time immemorial," says Tertullian (*ab immemorabili*), "as soon as we have emerged from the bath [of regeneration] we are anointed with the holy unction." Hence it may be doubted which sacrament was intended, or rather it is probable that it was intended to include both under the words which have been mentioned before, and referred to baptism—the verbs *accepit, percepit, consecutus est.*

There are but faint traces, so far as we know, of any other of the sacraments of the Church in the epitaphs of the early Christians in Rome. There is a monument placed under Column XIV. of the Lateran collection which was set up by the parents of one Œgrilius Bottus Philadespotus to their sweetest son, who died when he was a little more than nine

[margin: and of the Holy Eucharist,]

under the symbols of Bread and Fish.

years old. There is nothing in the inscription to indicate that the boy or his parents were Christian until we come to the end, when we see most carefully engraved an anchor, a fish, and a small circular loaf, marked on the top, in the old Roman fashion, with deep lines in the form of a cross, to facilitate its division. On another stone in the Kircherian Museum are engraved four similar loaves and two fishes underneath them. And the same symbols appear again on the following gravestone, which was found in Modena in 1862. De Rossi attri-

Bull., 1872, p. 100.

Bull., 1865, p. 76.

SYNTROPHION

butes this stone to the third century, and the Roman one is probably of the same date; for, from his intimate familiarity with ancient Christian monuments, he is able to certify that whereas we cannot tell how early the fish began to be used as a mystical symbol of the Christian faith, it had become extremely rare by the middle of the fourth century, and almost or altogether ceased by the beginning of the fifth. The same high authority does not doubt that this symbolical representation was intended to refer to the Holy Eucharist, that blessed sacrament which, having been the food of Syntrophion during life, now gave his surviving friends the sure hope of his resurrection to life everlasting.[1] For some of our readers this interpretation may require a few words of explanation.

They are probably already aware that from the earliest times the fish was an acknowledged symbol of our Blessed Lord. The initial letters of His name and principal titles (in Greek) made up the word ΙΧΘΥΣ, or fish:—

     Ι ΗϹΟΥϹ = JESUS
     Χ ΡΙϹΤΟϹ = CHRIST
     Θ ΕΟΥ = OF GOD
     Υ ΙΟϹ = SON
     Ϲ ΩΤΗΡ = SAVIOUR

---

[1] St. John vi. 55.

Points of Discipline and Practice.

And when once this had been pointed out, the fish became a sacred *tessera*, unintelligible indeed to the outer world, but highly valued and of most convenient use to the faithful, embodying, as it did, with wonderful brevity and distinctness a complete abridgment of the Creed—a profession of faith, as it were, both in the two natures, the Unity of Person and the Redemptorial office of our Divine Lord. Hence, Clement of Alexandria names the fish as one of the figures which might very properly be used on Christian seals, because " it contains in one name," as Optatus says,[1] " by means of its single letters, a whole multitude of holy names." But not only did the fish represent to the early Christians their Divine Lord; they considered that they were to resemble Him in this, as in all things else, and so themselves also were spoken of as little fish, because they received their new and spiritual birth in the element of water.[2]

As, therefore, the lamb stands, both in Holy Scripture and in early Christian art, both for Christ, " the Lamb of God, who taketh away the sins of the world," and for us Christians, who are " the people of His pasture, and the sheep of His hand," as the dove also sometimes represents the Holy Spirit, and sometimes those who are born of the Holy Spirit and in whom He dwells, so the fish in like manner denotes either one born again in the waters of baptism, or Christ, Who, as Origen says,[3] is figuratively called the fish. If the fish is engraved alone upon a tombstone, it may be doubtful which interpretation ought to be adopted; but if it is united with other symbols, as it usually is, the context will generally determine the sense. Thus, when we find ancient gems engraved with the figure of a ship on a fish's back, we can hardly be in error if we take it to mean Christ upholding His Church; or if a lamb or a dove occupy the place of the ship, we understand a Christian soul supported by Christ through the waves and storms of life. But when we find it united with bread, we know of no other sense that can

---

[1] Adv. Parmenianum, lib. iii. [2] Tertull., De Baptismo, 1.
[3] In Matt., Hom. xiii. 10.

be reasonably given to it than that of a Christian soul fed by the Holy Eucharist.

We need not trespass upon the domain of Christian art to find a justification of this interpretation, we will confine ourselves within the limits of our present subject—ancient Christian epitaphs; and of these there are two very remarkable specimens, the language of which will quite bear us out in all that we have said.

This interpretation confirmed by the epitaph of St. Abercius. Both of these epitaphs are written in verse, and their language is figurative; but for this very reason they are the better able to throw light upon the figures engraved on the tombstones, there being a natural affinity between the language of art and poetry.

The first is the epitaph of St. Abercius, Bishop of Hierapolis, a town situated within a few miles of Laodicea and Colossæ. Hence there was a Christian Church there from the very earliest times. St. Paul sends them his salutations in his Epistle to their neighbours at Colossæ,[1] and we have fragments of the writings of two of their Bishops even before St. Abercius, viz., Claudius Apollinaris and Papias. The last-named writer died about A.D. 170, and we are indebted to him for one of the earliest mentions of the Gospels which has reached us. Abercius seems to have lived not long after him, about the end of the second century. His epitaph has been long known, but was only imperfectly understood until recent discoveries of Christian monuments had thrown fresh light upon its mystical language.[2] The part of it which concerns our present subject is contained in a few lines towards its conclusion. Abercius has been describing his many and distant travels through Syria and to Rome, and he says—

Πίστις δὲ προῆγε,
Καὶ παρέθηκε τροφὴν Ἰχθύν τε μιῆς ἀπὸ πηγῆς
παμμεγέθη, καθαρὸν, ὃν ἐδράξατο παρθένος ἁγνή·
καὶ τοῦτον παρέδωκε φίλοις ἔσθειν διὰ παντὸς,
οἶνον χρηστὸν ἔχουσα, κέρασμα διδοῦσα μετ' ἄρτου·
. . . . . .
ταῦθ' ὁ νοῶν εὔξαιτο ὑπὲρ μου πᾶς ὁ συνῳδός.

---

[1] iv. 13.
[2] Spicil. Solesm., iii. 533; Acta SS. Bolland. Oct., tom. ix. p. 491.

Points of Discipline and Practice.

There are one or two unimportant variations in the reading of this text, and one or two words the translation of which is doubtful. The following translation omits none of these points that is of the least consequence. We translate, then, as follows :—" Faith led me on the road [or brought to me], and set before me for food fish from the one [or the sacred, or the Divine] fountain, the great and spotless fish which the pure Virgin embraced [or took in hand];[1] and this fish she gave to her friends to eat everywhere, having good wine, giving wine mixed with water, and bread. May he who understands these things pray for me." The allusion contained in the words, "the one fountain," need not be explained here; and all the rest is easily understood when once we recognise that the fish was used as a symbol of Christ in the Holy Eucharist; bread and wine and the fish come naturally together as the visible and invisible parts of one great mystery. Abercius is using a language which, whilst seeming enigmatical to the public, is (as he indicates in the last line) easily understood by the faithful throughout the whole world.

The second epitaph we have spoken of was discovered in 1839 in the ancient Cemetery of St. Pierre d'Estrier, near Autun, and its chronology has been made the subject of much critical discussion, some placing it as early as the time of the Antonines in the second century, others as late as the end of the fourth, and possibly even the fifth; whilst Cardinal Pitra, P. Secchi, P. Garrucci, and other learned authorities assign it to the earlier part of the third. De Rossi observes that the

and another epitaph found at Autun;

---

[1] Some understand by this pure Virgin our Blessed Lady, the mother of this mystical Fish; others understand Faith, which the early Christians often personified. We shall see in the next chapter one of the martyrs who, being interrogated about his parents, answered, "My true father is Christ; my true mother is faith in Christ" (see p. 140). The bread and the fountain are also brought together in a line of the Sibylline verses, vi. 15.—ἐκ δὲ μιῆς πηγῆς ἄρτου κόρος ἔσσεται ἀνδρῶν. And bread and the Blessed Virgin in i. 359. Pitra quotes in illustration an ancient title of our Blessed Lady, *fons Bethlemicus;* Bethlehem meaning the House of Bread.

characters in which it was written are not so old as the ideas which it expresses. Even these, however, he considers may possibly be earlier than the fourth century; but about the ideas there is a flavour of antiquity which cannot be mistaken, so that even some of those who believe that it was put together in its present form in the fourth century, think also that the particular part of it which has reference to the fish was probably as old as the days of St. Irenæus. The whole epitaph is too long to be inserted here; we quote only those fragments which concern our subject :—

> Ἰχθύος οὐρανίου θεῖον γένος,
> . . . . .
> Σωτῆρος δ' ἁγίων μελιηδέα λάμβανε βρῶσιν·
> Ἔσθιε, πῖνε, δυοῖν Ἰχθὺν ἔχων παλάμαις.

That is, it begins by calling upon Christians as "the Divine children or offspring of the Heavenly Fish," and then, after an allusion (in the intermediate lines which we have omitted) to their new and immortal life, received in the sacred waters which enrich the soul with wisdom, the writer goes on to bid them "receive the sweet food of the Saviour of the saints. Eat and drink, receiving, or holding, the Fish in your two hands;" which was at that time the mode of receiving holy communion.

These two epitaphs, from the East and the West, may be taken as proofs of the widely-spread use of the symbol of the fish in connection with the Blessed Sacrament of the altar, and justify us in contending that on the gravestones of the Catacombs the same symbol may not improbably have the same meaning. At the same time our readers must be on their guard against a foolish determination to find a hidden Christian meaning in everything painted or engraved on these ancient monuments, and a Christian sentiment in every word. We have known a modern author, interpreting these epitaphs, refuse to translate

> ΘΑΡΣΟΙΑΣ ΟΤ
> ΔΙΣ ΑΘΑΝΑΤΟΣ.

"Be of good courage; no man is immortal."

Points of Discipline and Practice. 137

He thought it more edifying to read, "[The son of] Tharsoiasus, twice immortal!" though he could not explain what was meant by it. And it is notorious how several writers, both at home and abroad, have been sorely puzzled to find a place in the succession of Roman Pontiffs, or among the Antipopes, for a man named Antimio, who died in the year 392, and who happened to be called in his (metrical) epitaph *Papas*. The epitaph was written by some one to whom Antimio had been foster-father, and he is therefore addressed in the first line as *Nutritor*, and in the fourth line he is called by an equivalent title *Papa!*

We do not know that anybody has been guilty of similar absurdities with reference to the interpretation of the fish and other symbols; but such a blunder might easily be made by one who was not aware of the various uses to which symbols were sometimes put by Christians as well as others. This will be pointed out in a future chapter. Meanwhile we only invite our readers to suspect an allusion to one of the sacraments when they find a fish engraved on a Christian monument in connection with water, and an allusion to another when they find it connected with bread. In both cases all the surrounding circumstances must be carefully taken into consideration before a decision is come to.

CHAPTER VIII.

THEIR MORAL AND SOCIAL ASPECT.

Interest of ancient inscriptions as records of mere human thought and feeling —Special interest of ancient Christian epitaphs—Acts of the Martyrs the only other records of the same period—Importance of these two witnesses when they agree, e.g., in omitting all mention of titles, parentage, country—Of slaves; freedmen; alumni; love of the poor; of labour; of chastity; innocence—Practical conclusions.

Interest of all ancient inscriptions,

"PLEASED as I was to meet with an old monument or statue in the course of my travels, I was much more delighted when I had the opportunity of reading a beautiful inscription. I felt as if a human voice was speaking to me out of the stone, sending its sound across long centuries of time, and crying out to men in the midst of the wilderness, 'You are not alone; other men have thought and felt and suffered before, like yourself.' If the inscription belongs to an ancient people that has perished, it conveys to the soul a certain sense of immensity, and awakens in us the thought of immortality, since it shows how ideas can survive the fall of empires."

especially if Christian.

If these remarks of a favourite French author of the last century express truly the feelings of educated men in the presence of ancient inscriptions, certainly no Christian can fail to take a lively interest in the inscriptions of the first ages of the Church. For these do not preserve to us the records of an extinct civilisation, or of a nation that has passed away, but of our own spiritual forefathers, of those with whom we have an intimate connection both in faith and feeling. We have already seen what dogmas of the faith these monuments bear witness to, more or less explicitly; in the present chapter we propose to speak of the less formal, but scarcely less interesting, subject of Christian thought and feeling. But, alas! as we have before observed, most of these epitaphs are too brief to give us the information we desire. It is here that we specially lament their laconic brevity. The dogmas of the faith are secured to us by the creeds and tradition of the Church, but the tone and temper of an age dies with it, and can only be recovered by a diligent study of its domestic records, which in the early Church consist mainly of epitaphs of the dead. One other class of documents there is belonging to the same period, to which we have occasionally referred — the Acts of the Martyrs; and where the testimony of these two witnesses is found to agree, whilst they differ from all similar documents of the same class belonging to the professors of other religions, their importance can hardly be called in question.[1] If, for example, they agree in withholding information on certain points on which the epitaphs and the judicial examinations of other men are wont to be communicative, we may confidently infer that the cause of this unusual silence is to be sought in the tenets of the Christian religion. *[Acts of the Martyrs only contemporary record of same kind.]*

Now, the judicial examination of men accused of any crime ordinarily begins with an inquiry as to their name, condition in life, worldly occupation, and other personal details. But on most of these points we find many of the martyrs and confessors of the faith were as obstinately reticent as their tombstones. They opposed to all questionings about them the short but comprehensive answer, "I am a Christian." Again and again they caused no little perplexity to their judges by the pertinacity with which they adhered to this brief profession of faith. The question was repeated, "Who are you?" and they replied, "I have already said that I am a Christian; and he who says that has thereby named his country, his family, his profession, and all things else besides." Or if they consented *[These witnesses agree on certain important points. L.B., i. pp. 120–130. E.g., silence about parentage, country,]*

---

[1] The examples which follow are taken only from Acts which are acknowledged as genuine by all critics.

to amplify their reply, the perplexity of the magistrates was only the more increased, for they seemed to speak insoluble enigmas. "I am a slave of Cæsar," they said, "but a Christian who has received his liberty from Christ Himself;" or, contrariwise, "I am a free man, the slave of Christ;" so that it sometimes happened that it became necessary to send for the proper official (the *curator civitatis*) to ascertain the truth as to their civil condition. If questioned about their parents, they denied that they had any, because Christ had said, "Call none your father upon earth; for one is your Father who is in heaven;[1] or they used symbolical language, and said, "Our Father is Christ, and our mother is the faith whereby we believe in Him." When brought face to face with their parents, and accused of falsehood, they replied, "Now I have fulfilled the law of Christ, which says, 'That except a man renounce father, and mother, and wife, and children for His name's sake, he is none of His.'" They owned no country as their native home, but "confessed that they were pilgrims and strangers on the earth," and that they were "seeking a better, a heavenly country;" that they were citizens of "that Jerusalem which is above, which was their mother."[2]

With these memories of the martyrs fresh in our mind, let us open any large collection of ancient epitaphs, or let us visit either the Lapidarian Gallery at the Vatican or the new selection in the galleries of the Lateran, and it is impossible not to be struck by evidence of the same characteristics pervading these also. What the martyrs habitually refused to answer to their judges is rarely or never to be found upon the epitaphs; and in these particulars there is the most remarkable contrast between Christian epitaphs and Pagan.

If we look into the index of any large collection of Pagan inscriptions, we find after the titles *servi* and *liberti* the word *passim;* that is to say, the mention of these two classes of society is so incessant, that it is useless to attempt to enumerate

---

[1] St. Matt. xxiii. 9.   [2] Heb. xi. 14; Gal. iv. 26.

Their Moral and Social Aspect. 141

the instances in which they occur. Among Christian inscriptions, on the other hand, we may almost say that we shall look in vain for the first of these titles, and with difficulty shall find the other. St. Paul had taught that under the new dispensation there was "neither bond nor free;" that "he that is called in the Lord, being a bondman, is the freeman of the Lord; and he that is called being free is the bondman of Christ."[1] *R.S.*, ii. And hence we find Christian men writing themselves down as slaves of God, but never slaves of their fellow-men. Aringhi, indeed, records an epitaph, *Hic situs Notatus servus fidelissimus;* but there is nothing to show that this too should not be understood in the same sense as having reference to the service of God. Bosio also has another which must certainly be the epitaph of a young Christian slave set up by his p. 437. masters :—

> FORTUNIONI BENEMERENTI
> QUI VIXIT ANNIS XVI. M.V.D. XV.
> FECERUN[T] DOMINI SUI IN PACE

"To the well-deserving Fortunio, who lived sixteen years five months fifteen days, his owners made this. In peace."

And Boldetti gives a third, the epitaph of a young girl, whose p. 385. parents record that out of charity they have given their liberty to seven slaves on the day of her funeral.

Of freedmen we have a few more notices, mainly of the same Rare mention indirect kind. One, whose patron had died and been buried of *liberti*. whilst he was absent, in the year 217, added on his return a *I.C.* few words on the side of the saracophagus, recording the day on which he had been "taken to God" (*receptus ad Deum*), and that this addition to the epitaph had been written by "Ampelius, a freedman." The whole monument had been erected by grateful freedmen—*Patrono piissimo liberti benemerenti sarcophagum de suo adornaverunt*—and it was only natural, therefore, that this Christian who added the date of

[1] Col. iii. 11 ; 1 Cor. vii. 22.

the death should mention that he too belonged to the same class. Three epitaphs in the Catacomb of St. Callixtus were in like manner the work of grateful freedmen, who (it would seem) must have been themselves also Christians. Possibly they had received their freedom from their Christian owners (in two instances ladies, in the other a gentleman) on occasion of their conversion, as we read in the Acts of St. Sebastian of some who, becoming Christians, gave liberty to their slaves, "because men who had begun to have God for their Father ought not to be the slaves of men."

L.M., xiii. 19.

AURELIO SCOLACIO PATRONO
DIGNISSIMO QUI VIXIT ANNIS LXX
IN PACE LIBERTI FECERUNT

R.S., iii. xxii. 2.

PETRONIÆ AUXENTIÆ C.F.
QUE VIXIT ANNIS XXX. LIBERTI FE
. . . NEMERENTI IN PACE.

R.S., i. xx.'3.

MARCIE RUFINE DIGNE PATRONE
SECUNDUS LIBERTUS FECIT.

"To Aurelius Scolacius, their most worthy patron, who lived seventy years, his freedmen made this. In peace."

"To Petronia Auxentia, a lady of senatorial rank (*clara femina*), who lived thirty years, well-deserving, her freedmen made this. In peace."

"To Marcia Rufina, a worthy patroness, Secundus, her freedman, made this."

The paucity of inscriptions of this class cannot be attributed to accident; it betrays the influence of Christian teaching, of which an ancient witness[1] wrote that it recognised no difference between slaves and masters, for that Christians call one another brethren for this very reason, because they account themselves to be all equal.

More frequent mention of *alumni*.

O.H., 2795, 4147, 4359.

There was another class of persons in ancient Roman society whose condition varied indeed very much according to the disposition of those into whose hands they fell, but in itself was essentially that of slavery; hence they are sometimes

[1] Lactant., Div. Instit., v. 14, 15.

coupled with the *liberti*, or provision is made in a last testament for their manumission. We speak of the *alumni*, or foster-children, most of whom were children who had been exposed by their inhuman parents, and being taken up by others, became their property. Everybody knows that even Greek philosophy counselled the murder of all misshapen children, and such as, being born of aged or diseased parents, did not promise to grow up strong and healthy citizens; and that the ancient Roman law gave a father the right of life and death within his own family. If, when a child was born, the father was unwilling that it should be brought up, it was either killed without pity, or sold, or exposed in some public place. This latter practice was discountenanced indeed, and even prohibited by the imperial laws, but Tertullian tells us that no law was evaded more easily, or with greater impunity. He even boldly challenges the very magistrates themselves, who were most forward in persecuting the Christians, and asks which of them can truly say that he had never made away with any of his own children, either by cold or hunger, or by drowning, or by throwing it to the dogs.[1] The common lot of children thus exposed was, we may be sure, either that they perished miserably, or that a still harder lot awaited them in the hands of odious speculators, who brought them up for their own selfish purposes to a life of slavery or sin. Pliny's letters to Trajan attest the frequency with which difficulties were apt to arise as to the legal *status* of these children. Trajan ruled that if it could be proved that they were the children of free parents they could not be held in bondage, nor even any demand made upon them for the refunding of the expense of their past maintenance. But in most cases it would not have been easy to supply such proof, so that they would be retained in slavery. Here then was a large and tempting field for the exercise of charity, of which we may be sure that the ancient Christians availed themselves as eagerly in Rome as is done to-day in

[1] Apolog., ix. ad Gentes i. 15.

China or other Heathen countries. It is not surprising, therefore, that we should find even in the small selection at the Lateran nearly a dozen epitaphs to the memory of these *alumni* or *alumnæ*, set up by their loving guardians; and in books we shall find very many more. Such epitaphs are not altogether wanting even in Pagan collections; but, as might have been expected, they are proportionately far more numerous among Christians. Sometimes the title only is given, without any epithet of affection, as in the following, from the Cemetery of St. Hermes :—

xiii. 20–31.

I.C., No. 56.

SEM VESTINO ALOM D V ID JAN
ACYNDINO ET PROC CONSS.

"To Semnus [or Sempronius] Vestinus, my foster-child, buried the 9th of January A.D. 340."

More commonly, there is at least the addition of some such word as *Dulcissimo*, and sometimes much more demonstrative tokens of affection, as in the following, *Alumno quem semper vice fili dilexit vivus posuit locus concessus a Cassia Afrodite*, where the affection which dictated the epitaph is more easily recognised than the grammatical construction of the words by which it is expressed. It seems to say that the place of burial was granted by one person and the epitaph written by another, who loved his *alumnus* in the place of a son. Another, in the Lateran Museum, says that he loved him tenderly, "*Quem amavit teneriter.*" A third, in the same collection, speaks still more strongly. Coritus loved the young Florentius, who died at the age of thirteen, "more than if he had been his own son" (*plus amavit quam si filium suum*): Coritus, however, is called not *patronus*, but *magister;* so probably Florentius was one of his pupils or apprentices (*discentes*) rather than a foster-child.

L.M., xiii. 23, 27.
C.I.L., iii. 2194.

xiii. 24; xvii. 3.

Christian charity.

For Christian charity was not confined within the limits of flesh and blood, or of accidental social relationship; it embraced the whole human race, and in an especial manner those whom the Pagan world had been wont most to despise and shun—viz., the poor and suffering. We have an indication of this in a title inscribed on an epitaph of the middle of the fourth century, which records the death of one Junianus, aged forty, who was buried on the 12th of April, A.D. 341; and his widow Victoria, who had lived with him for fifteen years from her virginity, records both of him and of herself that they were "lovers of the poor."

<small>Love of the poor.</small>

DEPOSSIO JUNIANI PRI IDUS APRILES MARCELLINO ET PROBINO
CONSS
QUI BIXIT ANNIS XL IN PACE DECISSIT ET AMATOR PAUPER-
ORUM BIXIT
CUM BRGNIA ANNIS XV BENEMERENTI BIRGINIA SUA BICTORA
BENEMERENTI FECIT AMATRIX PAUPERORUM ET OPERARIA.

The title of friend of the poor (*amicus pauperum*) is given in another epitaph to a Lector of the *titulus Fasciolæ* in Rome in the year 377; and in another set up at Milan, A.D. 486, a lady is called *amatrix pauperum*. To these may be added also a much more ancient inscription, found near the cathedral of Tharros, in Sardinia, to the memory of one who died at the age of sixty-five, and of whom his widow Clementia testifies that he was the dearest of friends, that he served the commandments of Christ in all things, and that he was a *præstator bonus pauperum*, which may be translated perhaps, "kind patron of the poor," unless (as De Rossi suggests) it be taken as the oldest example of the modern Italian *prestatore*, taken in a good sense, as one who "showeth mercy and lendeth."[1] In either sense it illustrates our present subject, and it may fairly be used for that purpose, as it undoubtedly belongs to the same period of time as the epitaphs of the Roman Catacombs, though it comes from a different country.

<small>Bull., 1873, p. 132.</small>

The first feeling which the sight of these epitaphs is likely to raise in the mind of a Christian, is a sense of their appropriateness as memorials of the disciples of Him who came to preach the Gospel to the poor, and showed Himself in so many ways their benefactor and friend. And next he would

<small>Alleged similar examples among Pagans examined.</small>

[1] Ps. xxxvi. 26.

probably reflect that such a title might be sought in vain amid the many thousands of Pagan epitaphs that have come down to us. Modern travellers,[1] however, tell us of a Pagan inscription of the second or third century, found in Asia Minor, in memory of one "who loved the poor for piety's sake" (τὸν πτωχοὺς φιλίοντα ἕνεκεν εὐσεβίης); and on another Pagan monument on the Appian Way between Rome and Albano an inscription invites the stranger to stop as he passes and to look at the tomb on his left hand, which contains the bones of a man "good, merciful, and loving the poor" (*boni, misericordis, amantis pauperis*).[2] Mommsen remarks that both the style and the sentiment of this inscription is eminently plebeian. The inscription itself records that the man's name was Euodius, and that he was a freedman of C. Atilius Serranus, and a fashionable jeweller in the Via Sacra.[3] A third inscription, at Beneventum, says of a Pagan nobleman, that "he loved everybody and was himself beloved by everybody" (*amanti omnium et amato omnibus*).

C.I.L., i. 224. *O.H.*, 7244.

I.R.N., 1431.

And besides these inscriptions, there are a few others breathing more or less the same spirit, inasmuch as they record what we should now call charitable bequests. One is of a doctor, or rather of an apothecary, a dealer in herbs and confections (*aromatarius*), who leaves to his son-in-law (who was in the same way of business) a small sum of money—about £50—and three hundred pots of his drugs and sweetmeats (*vascula dulciariorum*), in order that medical treatment may be supplied gratuitously to his poor and sick fellow-townsmen (*ægris inopibus*). A lady of Terracina founds an institution in memory of her son, in which 100 boys and girls are to

O.H., 114.

---

[1] Perrot et Guillaume, Exploration de la Galatie, p. 119.

[2] This is, of course, put for *pauperes*, just as we read on the medals of Augustus, *Ob civis servatos*.

[3] We say "fashionable" because the fact of residence in the Via Sacra is often recorded on monuments, as though it were specially honourable. Other localities similarly distinguished were the Circus Maximus and the Vicus Tuscus.

Their Moral and Social Aspect. 147

be fed for ever, each going out as soon as he has attained a *O.H.*, 6669. certain age—the boys at sixteen, the girls at fourteen—and all vacancies to be filled up at once, so that the number may always remain complete. And a gentleman of Atina, in the kingdom of Naples, leaves in like manner about £3000 for the maintenance of the children of his fellow-townsmen until they come of age, when they are to be sent out into the world, *I.R.N.*, 4546. each with the sum of about £8.

It is probable that these last bequests were direct imitations of the example which had been set by Trajan, who is usually accounted the first Imperial founder of institutions of this kind. Nerva, indeed, his predecessor, had made some movement in the same direction; but Trajan organised it on a much larger scale, extended it to all Italy, and provided for its permanence. It appears from an inscription found at Beneventum that in the first five years of his reign he made nine such foundations, which together provided for the support of nearly 14,000 children, and these were allowed to take the name of *Ulpiani*, in honour of their benefactor.[1] We know that his example was imitated not only by the best of his successors on the Imperial throne, but also by private individuals—*e.g.*, Pliny the younger, who both made a similar foundation himself, in lieu of the scenic or gladiatorial shows that were expected from him, and also exhorted his friends to do the same.[2]

Imperial benevolence imitated by private individuals.

The more obscure individuals whose epitaphs have been given above were probably moved by the same example, though Henzen would claim for the first of them (the jeweller's) an earlier date, for he assigns it to the Augustan age.[3] But what was the real motive of them all? Was it a genuine love for the poor? or was it mere patriotism, and a desire to benefit their country?

---

[1] Medals are extant of the *pueri et puellæ Faustiniani* of the years 153, 160, and 161, giving thanks to Faustina, the wife of Antoninus Pius, for a similar foundation.

[2] Ep. lib. i. 8; vii. 18.

[3] This antiquity is disputed by Egger, Memoires d'Histoire Ancienne et de Philologie, p. 355. Paris, 1863.

In the case of the Emperors and their officers, it is plain that the latter was the real motive. Pliny speaks distinctly of the *publica utilitas;* and in another epitaph, which has sometimes been referred to in connection with this subject, a gentleman who is praised for his lavish distribution of money is significantly qualified as "a lover of his fellow-citizens." But of Euodius, on the contrary, it is said that he was good and compassionate, "loving the poor." If he lived and died in the Augustan age, it must be allowed that his character presents a singular exception to that of the age in which he lived, and was even superior to the teaching of the higher schools of Pagan philosophy. Quinctilian tells us that Pity was honoured in Rome as a goddess;[1] yet Cicero, and Aristotle before him, had condemned it as a weakness;[2] and Virgil enumerates among the characteristics of his happy man,[3] that he neither suffered pain by pitying the poor, nor envy at the sight of the rich. At a later period, Seneca draws a line of distinction between the feeling of pity and the active habit of beneficence, and says that all good men will cultivate the one and avoid the other. For "What is pity?" he asks: "many praise it as a virtue, and call a good man compassionate" (which is just what the writer of this epitaph has done). "But pity is really a fault or vice of the mind; of a little mind giving way at the sight of other men's misfortunes; it is a weakness of mind—the wise man does not pity." "Nevertheless, he will come to the help of another man's tears though he takes no part in them (*occurret, non accedet*), he will stretch forth his hand to the shipwrecked, show hospitality to the exile, give a coin to the poor man, and divide his bread with the hungry."[4]

We need not stop to insist upon the essential difference between such beneficence as this and the charity of the Gospel, which bids us "rejoice with them that rejoice, and weep with them that weep."[5]

[1] V. xi. 38. [2] Cic., Tusc. Quæst., iv. 8; Aristot. de Rhet., ii. 8.
[3] Georg., ii. 499. [4] De Clem., lib. 2 cc. 4-6; De Benef., c. 95.
[5] Rom. xii. 15.

Their Moral and Social Aspect. 149

We conclude then that the two Pagan epitaphs which have been quoted, and which say of the deceased that they "loved the poor," are of a character altogether exceptional. The Greek one, indeed, being confessedly of the second or third century, was not improbably due to the secret influence of Christianity, which was insensibly changing the tone of men's thoughts, and guiding the world into an order of new ideas. "The world did not see the source of the change; it was hidden in the obscure retreats of the infant Church, but it was kept alive by the care and the charity of that new race of men who were receiving into their houses sick slaves cast away by their masters, infants exposed by their parents, and the poor who were dying of hunger at the doors of the wealthy men of Rome."[1] "In this way Christian charity, which so often in our own days leaves traces of itself in souls whence the light of faith has been withdrawn, seems also to have gone before faith in penetrating the darkness of Paganism, like that sweet and gentle light which both anticipates and survives the full brightness of the day."[2] That this was so, we have the most conclusive evidence that could be desired, the testimony of an enemy. "These cursed Galileans," writes Julian the Apostate to the Pagan *Pontifex Maximus*, "feed not only their own poor, but ours also whom they see uncared for;" and he goes on to insist on the necessity of imitating them in this trait of their character, if an effectual barrier was to be raised against the progress of the "new superstition."

The following inscription has been sometimes misunderstood as bearing upon the point before us. One who is new to the study of ancient epitaphs might not unnaturally imagine that the words *fecit bene* were intended to testify to the good works and active benevolence of this lady, Constantia, who had lived fifty years, and for whom the ancient acclamation, "Mayest thou live in Christ," is renewed in an artistic form. But the

The phrase Fecit bene explained.

---
[1] Villemain, De la Philosophie Stoique et du Christianisme, p. 62.
[2] Wallon, Histoire de l'Esclavage dans l'Antiquité, tom. iii. p. iii. c. i.

truth is, the inscription is incomplete: *fecit bene* is predicated not of Constantia, but of somebody else whose name it was intended to add, as the friend or relative who had buried her

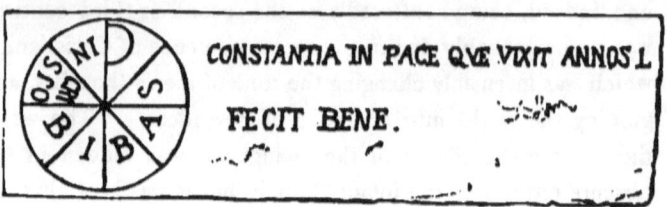

and set up her epitaph. For this is all that is meant by the words. We have seen *fecit* used in this sense in several epitaphs;[1] but *bene fecit* occurs also in some ten or twelve inscriptions of the Catacombs. It is expressed somewhat more fully in the following, found in 1843 in the Cemetery of St. Hermes:

Bull., 1873, p. 134.

GERONTIUS QUI VIXIT ANNOS XXV.
REMISIT AMUMNU NOMINE BENIGNU
QUI FECIT CORPORI BENE.

"Gerontius, who lived twenty-five years. He left behind him a foster-child by name Benignus, who fulfilled all the last offices for his body."

Bull., 1877, p. 96.

Or, as it is expressed in another epitaph found in the same place, "took care of his body," *curam corporis egit*. The phrase *fecit bene* occurs continually in this sense on the epitaphs of a Christian cemetery of the fourth or fifth century, lately discovered at Tropea, on the coast of Calabria.

Christian love of labour.

But to return to our Christian epitaph of A.D. 341. The widow of Junianus called herself not only a lover of the poor, but also *operaria*; and this, too, though a word of reproach among the Heathen, was an eminently Christian excellence. Cicero[2] couples the word *operarii* with *barbari*, using both as terms of ignominy. But we need not multiply proofs upon this point. It is notorious with what contempt the ancient Heathen world looked upon labour, especially manual labour. They deemed it the natural and inevitable lot of slaves, but altogether unworthy of a free man. From the Christian point

[1] See pages 119 and 142.   [2] Tusc. Quest., v. 36.

Their Moral and Social Aspect. 151

of view, on the other hand, it was the penalty of man's fall; but it was also a remedy for sin, and a condition of future reward. Even the Apostles themselves would "not eat any man's bread for nothing, but in labour and toil worked night and day, lest they should be chargeable to any," and they declared that "if any man will not work, neither let him eat." They "charged therefore and besought their disciples that, working with silence, they would eat their own bread."[1] This is not the only epitaph, therefore, in which this subject of praise is recorded; we find it on another in the newly discovered cemetery of St. Nicomedes in the Villa Patrizi, where a lady named Catianilla is called ἐργοποιός, and a third lady is said to have been *Laborum au[c]trix, castis socia.* *Bull.*, 1865. p. 53.

This last epitaph puts us in mind of another virtue which is specially commended in the ancient Christian epitaphs,— modesty and chastity; but of this we have already said enough in another place, and we have noted its recognition by the old Romans themselves. We may say the same also about love and concord, quietness and amiability, in husbands and wives. We will add, however, one more epitaph, illustrating the former subject, from the Cemetery of St. Callixtus :— Chastity.
Concord in married life.

   . . TATI VIRGINIÆ SUÆ PROBILIANUS
   QUEIUS FIDELITATEM ET CASTITATE ET BONITATE
   OMNES VICINALES EXPERTI SUNT, QUÆ
   ANNIS. N. VIII. ABSENTIA VIRGINI SUI SUAM CAS
   TITATEM CUSTODIVIT UNDE IN HOC LOCO SANCTO
   DEPOSITA EST III. KAL. FEBR. *R.S.*, iii., xxiv. 4.

" Probilianus to [Felici]tas, his wife from her virginity, whose fidelity, chastity, and goodness all her neighbours have known by experience; who preserved her chastity during the eight years' absence of her husband; wherefore she is buried in this holy place, the 30th of January."

The innocence of children, too, was made a theme of panegyric even on Pagan monuments; not so much, however, on its own account, perhaps, as a ground of complaint against the cruel fate which took them away so early from life. Moreover, in Christian epitaphs this quality is expressed under very pretty Innocence in children and others.

[1] 2 Thess. iii. 8–12.

figures, taken partly from Holy Scripture, partly from the writings of the Fathers, or rather (to speak more accurately) which are to be found in both those places alike. We have seen one child called "a little lamb of God."[1] Another title, used much more frequently, is "a little dove," "a dove without gall." This peculiar notion of natural history is mentioned both by St. Cyprian and Tertullian. The former says[2] that "the Holy Spirit came down in the shape of a dove, which is a simple and joyous creature, not bitter with gall;" and the latter[3] writes of it just as the epitaphs do, that it is "without gall." Hence it was taken as an emblem of simplicity, gentleness, and innocence, and used sometimes to stand for the Holy Spirit Himself, sometimes for a Christian soul, which is the temple of the Holy Spirit, just as we have seen that the very words themselves, *Spiritus Sanctus*, were used in the same double meaning. On an epitaph of the end of the third century, or beginning of the fourth, this title of "a dove without gall" is given to a noble lady, aged 66. The only other title given to her is "good" (*bona femina*). In the following inscription of the year 362, "goodness" is also predicated of a young lady, "a faithful virgin" (aged 20), "a dove without gall;" modesty too, and purity of faith:—

Margin notes: Expressed by figures and emblems. R.S., ii. p. 185. Bull., 1868, p. 7.

    MIRÆ BONITATIS SECUNDE
    QUÆ VIXIT PURA FIDE ANNOS
    VIGINTI PUDICA CESSAVIT
    IN PACE ID VIRGO FIDELIS
    BENEMERENTI QUIESCET ID JUL
    PALUMBO SINE FELLE. M. ET N.[4]

"To Secunda, of wonderful goodness, who lived with pure faith twenty years; modest; she died in peace, a faithful virgin, well-deserving. She died the 15th of July, a dove without gall."

---

[1] See page 33, No. 4. [2] De Unit. Eccles., c. ix. [3] De Baptismo, c. viii.
[4] De Rossi says that all practised in the interpretation of old monuments will recognise in these last letters the chronological notes of the consuls Mamertinus and Nevitta; and that the ID in the fourth line of the inscription was an anticipation (in error) of the same word in the next line, where it occurs in its proper place.

It remains to inquire whether these inscriptions throw any light upon the relations between Paganism and Christianity in its early beginnings; and De Rossi answers this question at once in the affirmative. He observes that one of the first accusations brought against "the new superstition" was "hatred of the human race." Tacitus tells us that it was for this that the Christians were condemned under Nero, and to us who know the religion of Christ as pre-eminently the religion of love, the accusation will always have sounded preposterous. Yet from the Pagan point of view it is not so hard to understand. In the mouth of a Roman statesman, or even an ordinary Roman citizen, during the first three centuries of our era, "the human race" meant only the existing social organisation of Roman civilisation; and this, it must be allowed, was threatened in its very foundations by the teaching of the Gospel. These brief epigraphical notices of its earliest professors make it clear how little account they made of the social bonds which held together that mighty and imposing fabric. *R.S.*, i. 342. Practical conclusion.

We have seen that the most striking point of contrast between the ancient Christian inscriptions and those of their Pagan contemporaries is, that the latter constantly set forth with accuracy the *status* of the person deceased, and therefore give his several names at least, if not his parentage also, and his titles; whilst the former, evidently of set purpose, or at least from some instinct which had the power and uniformity of law, omitted all these things as wholly without value. At first, indeed, in the very earliest infancy of the Christian society, the habit of recording the three names, or at least two, the *nomen* and *cognomen*, was not immediately and universally dropped, as we have seen by the specimens we have published from the Cemeteries of Prætextatus and of the Via Nomentana. But already the new and more simple nomenclature had been begun, and before long it came into universal use. We do not mean that there was any written or even traditional law upon the subject; it was the spontaneous effect of the new religious doctrines gradually leavening the whole thoughts and feelings of those who embraced them, and leaving its impress, more or less distinct, on every detail of their daily lives. It was quite possible, therefore, that here and there a few neophytes, or persons not yet thoroughly impregnated with the Christian spirit, might depart from the usual practice; or the same thing might happen through inattention, or from some other special cause. In this way we account for the rare instances in which either slavery on the one hand, or noble blood on the other, finds a record in the epitaphs of the Catacombs. But the general rule is plain, and diametrically opposed to such a record. The Christian doctrine upon the subject is reflected in the great bulk of Christian epigraphy as in a mirror.

CHAPTER IX.

INSCRIPTIONS WITH SYMBOLS.

Epitaphs with symbolical ornamentation—Three classes of symbols—I. Religious: The Good Shepherd, Noe's ark, dove, fish, anchor, peacock, lighthouse, crowns, horse, cross, monogram in varieties of form, crux gammata—II. Civil: Marble cutters, carpenter, blacksmith, fisherman, dentist, surgeon, soldier; III. Nominal: Pagan as well as Christian. Examples.

BESIDES the common mode of writing in letters of the Greek and Latin alphabets, the early Christians made use of another peculiar to themselves—secret and hieroglyphical, so to speak—by means of images, signs, and symbols. Three columns at the Lateran Museum (XIV.–XVI.) are given up to epitaphs of this class; and they are very interesting. There are three principal families of them; the first may be called religious, as the symbols have reference to Christian doctrine; the second—civil—denoting the trade or profession which was followed by the deceased during his life; and the third—nominal—being only a pictorial rendering of his name. {Three classes of symbols on epitaphs.}

The first is by far the most numerous, and most deserving our attention. There are ten specimens in our page of selections; and four of these (Nos. 2, 12, 13, and 15) contain figures of the Good Shepherd. This was quite the favourite subject of representation with the early Christians; it continued to be the leading type and most characteristic sample of Christian art all through the ages of persecution. Tertullian[1] tells us that it was often designed upon chalices. We see it ourselves painted in fresco upon the roofs and walls of {(1.) Religious. The Good Shepherd.}

[1] De Pudicitia, cc. vii. x.

Epitaphs of the Catacombs.

Inscriptions with Symbols.

1. To Mæcius Aprilis, a maker of images, who lived twenty-seven years, two months, five days. To him, well-deserving, in peace.

2. Zosimus to Adolius [Anatolius?], his sweetest son, who lived twenty years — months three days.

3. Pontius Leo during his lifetime made this for himself; and Pontia Maza. . . . They made this for their well-deserving son Apollinaris.

4. Bauto and Maxima made this during their lifetime.

6. Elpis and Cyriace made this.

7. Epictetus and Felicia, his parents, made this for their sweetest, well-deserving son Felix, who lived fourteen years seven months eighteen days. May Christ receive thee in peace.

8. Porcella sleeps here in peace, who lived three years ten months and thirteen days.

9. Elis and Victoria, her parents, to their well-deserving daughter, who lived two years three months. In peace.

10. Antissius Crescentianus and Antisius Genialis, his sons, wrote this for their father, Antissius Crescens, who lived sixty-seven years.

11. Ælia Victorina set this up to Aurelia Proba.

12. Florentius. In peace.

13. Aurelius Castus [who lived] eight months. Antonia Sperantia [made this] for her son.

14. Severa, mayest thou live in God.

15. Sabinus to his well-deserving wife Celerina, who lived fifty-five years six months and fifteen days. In peace.

16. To the well-deserving Asellus, who lived six years eight months and twenty-eight days.

the sepulchral vaults and more spacious chambers of the Catacombs; roughly carved on innumerable gravestones, or more carefully sculptured on sarcophagi; traced in gold upon glass, moulded on lamps, engraved on rings; in a word, represented on every species of Christian monument that has come down to us. Neither need we say anything in explanation of its meaning or to justify its use. We will only note the singular appropriateness of such a figure on the tombs of the dead, who had now been received to their last home, and were housed for ever in the heavenly fold, secure from all fear and danger. "Carried home on the shoulders of the Good Shepherd" are the words used concerning the dead in one of the prayers of an old Roman sacramentary; and it is the same idea which was present to the minds of those who traced these rude figures on the gravestones. We add another specimen of the Good

Shepherd from the Cemetery of St. Callixtus, though some persons have preferred to see in this only a literal representation of the man named on the epitaph, as of his wife in the *orante.* It appears from the inscription that the husband (named Moses) procured the grave during his lifetime for himself and his wife; but, though it is very possible that he may have intended the figure of the woman in the attitude of prayer to be some sort of representation of his departed wife, it is

Inscriptions with Symbols. 159

incredible that he should have ventured to use for himself a figure consecrated by long and universal usage to our Blessed Lord. It is less easy to account for the next figure, from the same cemetery, where a woman takes the place of the shepherd; and we shall not attempt in this place to give any explanation of it. We will only mention that these *oranti*

(as they are called), though almost always female figures, are yet found sometimes on the graves of men, the disembodied soul being the idea present to the artist, rather than the person deceased. *Bull.*, 1868, p. 13.

Next to the Good Shepherd, Noe's ark is the subject which Noe's ark. occurs most frequently in our page of specimens (Nos. 7, 9, and 15). It is always represented in one form, and that removed as far as possible from historical truth. Instead of a huge vessel riding upon the waves, containing eight persons, together with a vast multitude of living animals, we see a single individual standing in a small box, with a dove, bearing an olive branch, flying towards him; and this individual is often not a man, but a woman; once her name is added, the name of the deceased on whose gravestone it was painted— Juliana. The meaning of this is quite obvious. "Nobody doubts," says St. Augustine[1]—and Tertullian and St. Cyprian had said the same before him—"Nobody doubts that the Church was typified in the ark of Noe, though this might have appeared a mere conjecture of man's imagination, had not the Apostle Peter expressly declared it in his Epistle."[2] The survivors, therefore, of Juliana, and of every other person buried in the Catacombs on whose tombs this story was told, meant to express their sure faith and hope that their departed friend, having been received into the Church by baptism, and lived a faithful member of it, had died in the peace of God, and had now entered into his rest.

Thus the dove with the olive branch was in fact equivalent to what we have seen to be one of the most common written epitaphs, *Spiritus tuus in pace*. But there was also another form of this epitaph, *Spiritus tuus in pace et in Christo;* and this too is exactly expressed pictorially, when the dove is found with the monogram, as in the following, which is at the end

Bull., 1874, p 65.

of an inscription on the *mensa* of an *arcosolium* in the Cemetery of St. Soteris, or with the fish, as on a stone found in the most

Bull., 1864, p. 9

ancient part of the Catacomb of St. Priscilla, without any words at all. In another from the same place, the dove seems to have been added, as a sort of afterthought, by way of correcting in some degree the blunder of the fossor who had fixed the stone in its place upside down.

[1] De Unit. Eccl., 9.   [2] I., iii. 20, 21.

Inscriptions with Symbols. 161

Of course the dove was primarily (as being suggested by the manifestation at our Lord's Baptism) a type of the Holy Ghost. But this did not in any way militate against its being used also

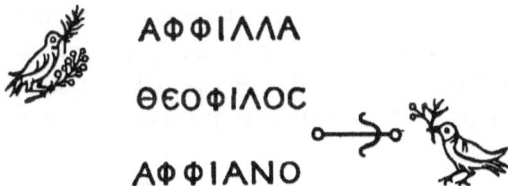

as an emblem of a Christian soul. On the contrary, as the very name and title of the Holy Spirit was given to those souls in whom He dwelt (of which we have seen several examples), so it was only natural that there should be the same double use of the symbols also. Sometimes, therefore, the dove appears on the gravestones side by side with the words *Palumbulus sine felle*, or with its equivalent, *Anima innocens*, *anima simplex*, &c. In one epitaph, belonging to a double grave, the names of the deceased are written over the heads of two doves, Beneria and Sabbatis. In another, a dove sits on the mast-head of a vessel, and around its head is written, " Whose soul has been received by God " (*Cujus spiritus a Deo acetus est*, for *acceptus*). Sometimes it is represented with the palm branch in addition to the olive, or instead of it—*i.e.*, the idea of victory is introduced as well as peace.

I.C., p. 421.
Bull., 1864, p. 11.
R.S., iii. p. 11.

ΑΦΦΙΛΛΑ
ΘΕΟΦΙΛΟC
ΑΦΦΙΑΝΟ

" Affilla Theophilus to Affianus."

Sometimes the same idea is suggested by carving the dove with a wreath or crown in its beak; and De Rossi quotes very appositely (from the genuine Acts of certain Greek vir-

L

gins who suffered martyrdom at Corinth, which have been recently published by Cardinal Pitra), a vision, in which one of them saw on the night before their martyrdom the Holy Ghost coming down from heaven bearing the crown of victory, to strengthen and encourage her for the conflict. Sometimes the dove is drinking out of a vase, or pecking at grapes, as

though to denote the soul's enjoyment of the fruits and refreshing streams of eternal happiness in Paradise.[1] In a word, the representations of the dove on the tombstones of the Catacombs are simply innumerable, and they occur in every variety of position and action, none of which are at all difficult to understand.

The anchor.

xvi. 45, 46.

In No. 6 of our selection an anchor appears on the epitaph of a double grave, in which one of the persons buried had the name of Elpis, or Hope. It appears also on other stones in the Lateran Gallery, and in a large number of ancient Christian epitaphs collected in books, belonging to persons bearing this same name, either in Latin or Greek, and in some one or other of its forms—Spes, Elpis, Elpidius, Elpizusa. Moreover, these epitaphs are found to be specially numerous in the most ancient parts of the Catacombs. And indeed St. Paul's Epistle to the Hebrews,[2] and the instruction of Clement of Alexandria,[3] are sufficient to satisfy us both as to the meaning of this symbol, and also the antiquity of its use. Sometimes it was so formed, evidently by design, as to suggest to the Christian eye the idea of the Cross, the very foundation of Christian hope; and in some epitaphs it is united with the fish in a very striking and significative way. Indeed, these two symbols are found together

Fish.

[1] See St. Aug., Conf., ix. 3.   [2] vi. 19.   [3] Pædagog., iii. 106.

on more than twenty gravestones of the Catacombs, to say nothing of engraved gems, in which class of monuments they are almost inseparable. Perhaps it was the connection of both of them with the sea which caused this association of ideas. Anyhow the result is most happy, for it becomes equivalent to those words so often inscribed on the earliest epitaphs, SPES IN CHRISTO, SPES IN DEO, SPES IN DEO CHRISTO. The only difference is that in the one case the idea is expressed alphabetically, in the other by hieroglyphics; and the latter has this advantage over the other, that it suggests also the idea of the Cross, apart from which Christian hope has no foundation.

We have already explained the double meaning of the fish, and in this example, the combination of the fish (in

its secondary sense) with the anchor is very suggestive of Christian thought. It brings to our minds the words of our Blessed Lord, that "when He was lifted up on the Cross, He would draw all men unto Him;" the fish are here Christian souls swimming towards that which is the centre and loadstone of their affections, the Cross of Christ. Sometimes other symbols are united with the anchor in a less striking way, though doubtless not without a definite hidden meaning on the part of those who inscribed them; as in this, from the very ancient crypt of Lucina; the union of the cross-shaped anchor, the sheep and the dove, seems to proclaim one of the fold of Christ redeemed by His Cross, in which he had placed all his hope, and now released from the bonds of the flesh and entered into everlasting rest. Still more numerous symbols are crowded together on the next, which is probably quite as ancient as

164   *Epitaphs of the Catacombs.*

the last, if not more so. It is engraved on the centre of a sarcophagus which was found near the Confession of St. Peter.

Bull., 1873, tav. v.

In modern times it had formed a part of the Campana Collection, whence it has found its way to Paris.

Peacock.

Lighthouse.

Other symbols more rarely used are such as the peacock in No. 11, which was a recognised emblem of immortality; and the ship approaching a lighthouse in the following (and in an-

Inscriptions with Symbols. 165

other which stands next to this in the Lateran Museum). This seems intended to suggest the idea that the soul of the

deceased is like a ship which has escaped all the perils of its voyage, and is now happily entering the haven of rest.

Another subject more frequently repeated is of wreaths, Crowns. garlands, and crowns, either alone or held in the beaks of birds; and on other Christian monuments, *e.g.*, on the gilded

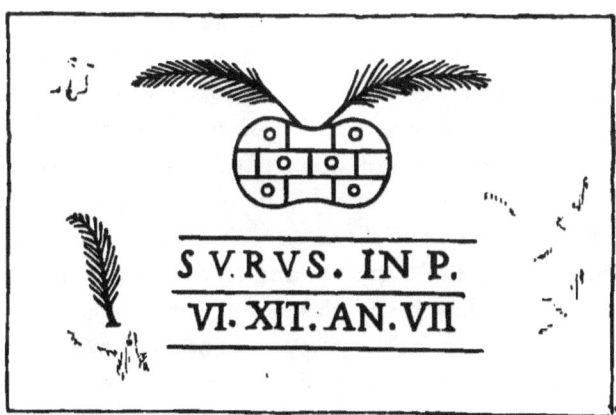

glasses of the fourth century, held over the heads of the saints by our Blessed Lord, or (in mosaics) by the hand of God issuing out of a cloud. All these have manifest reference to the prizes awarded to successful athletes and other competitors in the Pythian and Olympic games, and to the corresponding labours and contests against spiritual enemies which make up the trial of a Christian life. It is only a pictorial representation of the same symbolical language that is used more than once by St. Paul; as when he bids his Corinthian converts "so run that they may obtain," or instructs St. Timothy that "he that striveth for the mastery must strive lawfully," or says concerning himself, that he has "fought a good fight and finished his course, so that there is now laid up for him a crown of justice, which the Lord, the just judge, will render to him in that day, and not only to him, but to them also that love His coming."[1]

Horse.
L.M., xv. 51.

Bull., 1867, p. 82; 1873, p. 69.

The same explanation must be given also of the representation of a horse, which appears on a few Christian monuments; a horse at full speed running towards a palm branch or to the monogram of Christ. And it was doubtless under the influence of the same idea that the name Agathopus, "excellent of foot," became a favourite among the faithful. This view of the Christian life was likely to be specially present to men who were familiar on the one hand with the continual races, wrestlings, and other contests of athletes, and the gladiatorial combats; and, on the other hand, lived from day to day in constant apprehension of being called upon to confess the faith in the face of tortures and death itself, often in the same arena.

Cross.

Another symbol (so to call it) of which we must give some account is the sign of the cross. We need not quote the well-known passages of Tertullian and others which show the love of the early Christians for this sign of our salvation, and their frequent use of it. They were said to be *crucis religiosi*,[2] and it was known as the *signum Christi, signum immortale, signum cæleste Dei*, τὸ κυριακὸν σημεῖον.[3] But there were obvious reasons why it should not be fully exposed to public gaze before an unbelieving world. Death by means of a cross was specially ignominious as being a punishment reserved for slaves; and

---

[1] 1 Cor. ix. 24; 2 Tim. ii. 5, iv. 7. [2] Apolog. c. 16.
[3] Clem. Alex. Stromata, vi. 11; Lactant. de Mort Persec., cc. x. xliv..

Inscriptions with Symbols. 167

the famous caricature of the Crucifixion, scratched on a wall on the Palatine, is a sufficient proof of the use the Pagans were likely to make of this corner-stone of the Gospel history when brought before them. Nevertheless, where Christian symbols were used at all, it would have been hard to exclude this in some form or other.

We have already mentioned that the anchor was often so fashioned on ancient Christian epitaphs as to suggest this form to an instructed mind. A similar use seems to have been made of the trident also; certainly of the forms of the masts and yards of a ship, and of the sticks or stems among garlands of flowers. But these belong to the paintings rather than to the epitaphs of the Catacombs. A form under which it appears in inscriptions is the letter T. Tertullian, quoting Ezech. ix. 4, *Signa Tau super frontes*, &c., says: "Now the Greek letter Tau and our own T is the very form of the cross, which he predicted should be the sign on our foreheads in the true Catholic Jerusalem."[1] Hence we see examples of this in the Catacombs—*e.g.*, in an inscription IRETNE, lately dis- *Bull.*, 1863, covered in a part of the Catacomb of San Callisto, belonging *R.S.*, ii. 319. to the third century, and in another from the same place,

ΑΦΡΟΔΙϹΙϹ
T

and also in the monogram of TYRANIO on a sarcophagus; in

which the prominence given to the letter T evidently has a symbolical significance. We even find the letter itself in-

---

[1] C. Marc., iii. 22. The number 300 being expressed in Greek by this letter Tau, came itself, even in apostolic times, to be regarded as equivalent to the cross. See Barnab. Ep. Cath., c. 9, ed. Hefele, p. 22.

scribed alone, or in combination with the letter P, on a tombstone.

In the most ancient part of the lowest *piano* in the crypts of Lucina we meet with a grave with the inscription

ΡΟΤΦΙΝΑ
ΕΙΡΗΝΗ

with a simple equilateral cross (*a*) beneath the latter name. The same sign is virtually contained also in the figure *b*, which

occurs on an inscription of the year 268 or 279, as well as upon others not bearing certain dates. But this was probably intended merely as a combination of the first letters of the two words Jesus Christ in Greek, I X, and was therefore rather a compendious form of writing than a symbol properly so called.

R.S., ii. 330.
I.C., p. 16.

Monograms.

The Constantinian monogram, as it is commonly called (*c*), formed of the first two letters of the Greek word for Christ, the X with the P, seems to have been used at first in the same way, merely as a contracted form of the name, even before the triumph of Constantine. It is true that the few dated inscriptions before that event do not supply us with any specimen of it. But it has been found scratched on the plaster side by side with the earlier forms (*a* and *b*), both in San Callisto and the Catacomb of St. Agnes, in galleries which bear every sign of being prior to the time of Constantine. It is also found engraved in inscriptions, and nearly always under such circumstances that it cannot be treated as a merely ornamental addition, but must be read as an integral part of the inscription—*e.g.*, VIVAS IN DEO ET ☧, DEO SANCTO ☧ UNI, &c. Other Greek names were not unfrequently abridged at this time into monogrammatic signs; and why should not the names of Christ have been similarly treated?

Inscriptions with Symbols. 169

This form of the monogram, and also the simple Greek cross, appear on the coins of Constantine; and after his time we meet with the modifications of it *d*, *e*, and *f*, but especially the latter, which became the recognised triumphal form of the cross. It was a slight modification of a wáy of writing the Greek Rho, which is met with on some old Greek inscriptions and on medals of Herod the Great. In some instances the figure is reversed as in *g*, or placed obliquely as in *h* and *i*, but these were probably due to individual caprice, and had no special meaning. From the middle of the fourth century, it is usually flanked on either side by the letters Alpha and Omega. Once or twice we find on tombs in the Catacombs a monogram formed from the union of ☧ and the letter N, being intended, apparently, for the initials of the words ΧΡΙCΤΟC ΝΙΚΑ, *Christ conquers*, and belonging, of course, to post-Constantinian times.

A form of the cross (*k*) which is sometimes found both in paintings and on epitaphs after the middle of the third century is composed of a fourfold repetition of the Greek Γ; and because the symbol thus formed was in use among the Brahmins, Buddhists, and in other Oriental superstitions, some French writers have attempted to establish an historical connection between them and the Christian religion. It has been demonstrated, however, by De Rossi, that this *crux gammata*, as it is called, was no stranger even in Western Europe. It is found on Greek coins in Corinth and in Sicily, and was in a Samnite tomb, and in Rome itself. It was no spontaneous invention of the early Christians, no fruit of their own traditions; neither did they borrow it from any Oriental source. It was in use in their neighbourhood, and they gladly availed themselves of it, as of any other disguised forms of a figure so dear to them, which yet they did not dare to display openly. In Italy, they did not begin to use the plain Latin cross till about the beginning of the fifth century. In Africa, however,

Bull., 1873, p. 60.

Crux gammata.

R.S., ii. 318.
Bull., 1868, p. 91.

it had been used much earlier, and by the end of the sixth century it was very common everywhere.[1]

Besides mere artistic symbols, Scriptural histories are also sometimes figured on the tombstones of the Catacombs, but of course in a very condensed form, and by allusion rather than by actual representation, and with the same reference to their doctrinal meaning; the resurrection of Lazarus, for example, or a scene from the history of Jonas, as prefiguring and giving us an assurance of our own resurrection. It is not so easy to suggest the reason for selecting the scene depicted on No. 14, the adoration by the wise men of the Holy Child Jesus on His Mother's knee. But in the representations of SS. Peter and Paul in No. 16, of which there are four or five other examples in the Lateran Museum, there is no doubt that the survivors desired to recommend the deceased to the prayers of those apostles, that they might be made worthy to enter into their company. They were an equivalent to those acclamations we have seen addressed in words to others of "the noble army of martyrs."

xiv. 42-47.

(2.) Civil.

The second, but by no means so numerous a class of symbolical representations on the tombstones of the Catacombs, has no reference to the Christian faith of the deceased, but only to his profession or occupation in the world during life. Thus Mœcius Aprilis (in No. 1 of our selection), who was buried in the Cemetery of Cyriaca, was both called a maker of statues or images in the inscription, and we should have gathered the same from the instruments of his labour which are figured at either end of the epitaph. The same instruments must have been intended to tell the same story in No. 2 also, whilst the saw and hatchet in No. 4 seem rather to denote a carpenter. The bellows and anvil in No. 5 manifestly belong to a blacksmith; and another example of the same trade, similarly represented, has been found in the Cemetery of St. Callixtus. We can hardly be wrong in conjecturing that Antissius Crescens,

Sculptor.

Carpenter.
Blacksmith.
R.S., ii, xlv. 55.

Fisherman.

[1] De Rossi, De Titulis Carthag. apud Spicil. Solesmn., iv.

Inscriptions with Symbols. 171

whose two sons set up the inscription No. 10, was a fisherman. Other inscriptions of the same kind in the Lateran Museum set before us a carder of wool, a marble-cutter, a dealer in corn or a baker—the symbol is a measure of corn—and representatives of some other trades, not all of which, however, can be determined with certainty.

Fabretti has preserved to us from one of the Catacombs the monument of a maker of sarcophagi, to which De Rossi says it is impossible to assign a date later than the third century.

R.S., iii. 443. Maker of sarcophagi.

On it is represented a man in the act of making some of the ornamental work of a sarcophagus with a pointed instrument, which a boy is rapidly turning by means of a strap or cord, the two ends of which are in his hands. A finished sarcophagus of a smaller size stands by, with the name Eutropus upon it in Greek letters. It is worth observing that on neither of these sarcophagi is there any Pagan figure; on one there are only the spiral or wavy lines common on such monuments, and two lions' heads; and the other is still plainer, the name and four swimming dolphins. But the Christian profession of the sculptor is put beyond question by the dove with the olive branch in the corner, and an inscription, in which the son of Eutropus, who made the monument, calls his father holy, and " a worshipper of God," and adds the Christian formula *In pace*.

In the recent excavations round the Basilica of San Lorenzo *fuori le mura* part of an inscription came to light, engraved on a very heavy stone, which certainly never closed a grave in the

Surgeon.

Catacombs, but must have belonged to the cemetery above ground. Nevertheless we give a figure of it here for the sake of the instruments which are upon it. The inscription tells us

of some person whose name ended in *inus* (Victorinus, Celerinus, or some other), who during his lifetime made this tomb for himself at his own expense,[1] and then the two instruments are engraved which our readers see. In one of them it is impossible not to recognise another example of an instrument which had been found in 1714 on the gravestone of one Alexander, in the Cemetery of Calepodius, and concerning

Dentist.

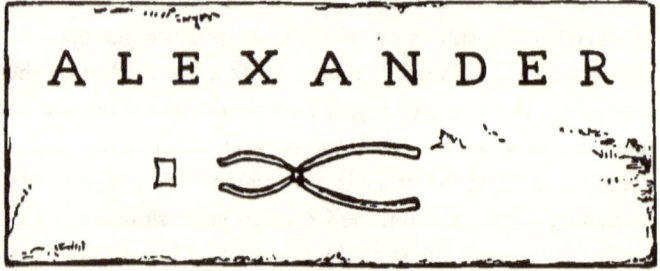

which Boldetti had conjectured that it might not possibly be meant for an instrument of martyrdom. He acknowledged, however, that this was very doubtful, and immediately went on to produce other inscriptions in which the emblems or imple-

[1] ἑαυτῷ ΑΙΠΟΙΗϹΑ for ἐποίησα.

ments of different trades were represented. We think he may very well be excused for not recognising a dentist's forceps and the tooth which it had extracted, and that the whole inscription was simply equivalent to "Alexander, the Dentist." But in the other example, the tooth appears still grasped by the successful instrument, and another instrument of a dentist's profession is by its side. In 1851 De Rossi was present when a stone was dug out of the Cemetery of Pretextatus, which had closed a Christian grave fifteen hundred years before, and on it, instead of a name, was a representation of a whole case of surgical instruments, amongst which the same two appear; and

then, to complete the demonstration, De Rossi is able to add that he has seen the very same case of instruments engraved on an ancient monument in Palestrina, to the memory of one P. Ælius Pius Curtianus, who is expressly called a *medicus*.   O.H., 7426.

This was a Pagan monument, and other similar representations are to be found in all large collections of monuments of any class, as they are the mere reflection of civil and social life—*e.g.*, on how many English monuments do we find the sword, the gun, and the banner as the insignia of military service, or an anchor on the tombs of sailors, a palette and brush on the painters', &c. Still it is certainly not altogether in harmony with the spirit which dictated the great bulk of the epitaphs in the Catacombs; for, as a general rule, all mention of worldly interests and occupations is as rigorously excluded from these as titles which minister to pride and vanity. There will always be some exceptions, however, to these rules; and in his last volume of "Roma Sotterranea" De Rossi has given us from an *arcosolium* in the Cemetery of St. Callixtus the picture of a woman standing surrounded with benches and tables covered with vegetables, which he interprets as indicating the nature of her business followed during life by the person whose tomb it ornaments; and Bosio had long since given us an epitaph from the Cemetery of Domitilla of a woman "who sold barley in New Street" (*vendidit horreum de Biâ Nobâ*).

Whilst upon the subject of trades and professions recorded on Christian tombstones, it is worth mentioning that there was discovered a few years ago in the Villa Patrizi, outside the Porta Pia, a small subterranean cemetery, which De Rossi was almost disposed to believe was peculiar to Christian soldiers, the barracks being situated at no great distance. One of the inscriptions, scratched apparently with some iron instrument by the inexperienced hand of a comrade, ran as follows:—

<small>Soldiers.</small>

<small>*Bull.*, 1865, p. 49.</small>

> [DION]ISIUS MILIX COH S(EXTÆ?)
> STUS FRATER FRATRI
> EMERENTI FOSUIT QUI V
> ANNIS XXX IN JACE.

He observes that the barbarisms on the epitaphs of the Pagan members of the Prætorian Guard were hardly less glaring or frequent than on this fragment of a Christian epitaph. He also says that he has found several other inscriptions of Christian soldiers, which is only what we should have expected from the distinct testimony of Tertullian, whilst yet a Catholic, that Christians were to be found both in the army and navy. "We sail with you," he says, when addressing his Apology to heathen readers, "and we fight with you;" and in another place he enumerates the camp in the list of places which were already full of Christians, "leaving nothing to the undisturbed possession of the heathen except their temples and theatres."[1]

(3.) Nominal.   The third class of symbolical representations is almost too trifling to deserve mention; but it has always found favour with some persons, whether Pagan or Christian, Greek or

---

[1] Apol., cc. 37, 42. See also De Coronâ, i.

Inscriptions with Symbols.

Roman. We allude to those which are merely nominal, or figured representations of the name.

It was not at all an uncommon practice among the old Romans to choose a device or a trade-mark on this principle— *e.g.*, tiles or terra-cotta vessels made on the estates of Flavius Aper (*ex prædiis Fl. Apri*) are marked with a wild boar, and those of Stephanus with a crown. They did the same also on their sepulchral monuments. [Used by Pagans in Greece and Rome.]

An inscription on a Pagan sepulchre on the Via Appia, to the memory of one M. Antonius M. L. Philomusus, adds after this last name the monosyllable *mus*, as though this had been its familiar abbreviation, and then carves at the side two figures of a mouse (*mus*).[1] In the same way in Athens the tomb of one Leo is ornamented with a lion; so in the Roman Catacombs was the epitaph of one Pontius Leo (in No. 3 of our selection), and a little pig is added to that of a child named Porcella (in No. 8). Boldetti gives one with the figure of a donkey, the man's name being Onager; and Marangoni[2] another, *Spiritum Caprioles in pace*, with the figure of a goat at the side. And in the following example the ship seems to have been selected as the *signum* or token whereby the parents might recognise the grave of their daughter, aged sixteen, because of its connection with her name, Navira. [Christian examples. p. 428.]

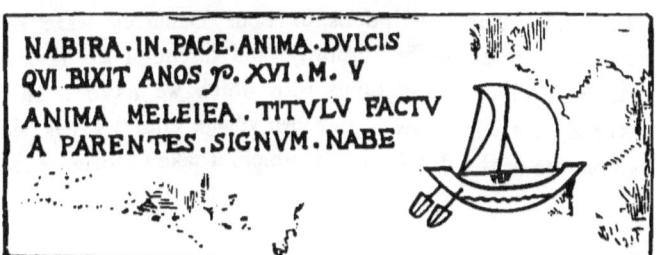

NABIRA·IN·PACE·ANIMA·DVLCIS
QVI BIXIT ANOS J°. XVI . M. V
ANIMA MELEIEA . TITVLV FACTV
A PARENTES . SIGNVM . NABE

"Navira, in peace, a sweet soul, who lived sixteen years five months, a soul sweet as honey. The epitaph is put up by her parents. The sign a ship."

---

[1] Pitture e sepolcri scoperti sull' Esquilino nell' 1875. Par Eduardo Brizio, p. 25.
[2] Acta Sti. Victorini, p. 102.

CHAPTER X.

CONCLUSION.

Inscriptions of Pope Damasus—Chief characteristics of Christian epitaphs, their hopefulness—They reflect contemporary history and general state of Christian thought and feeling at different periods—Ancient Christian epitaphs in other countries; Great Britain, Spain, and Gaul—Conclusion.

Inscriptions of Pope Damasus.

THERE was once a very interesting class of inscriptions in the Catacombs (and one or two specimens, as well as a few fragments of some others, may still be seen there), to which we have scarcely made any allusion in these pages; those, we mean, which were set up on the tombs of the martyrs by Pope Damasus in the latter half of the fourth century. They are in every point of view of great value and importance, and deserve a treatise by themselves; but they can hardly be called epitaphs, in the usual acceptation of the word, and the consideration of them belongs rather to the history of the Catacombs than to that branch of the subject which we have been handling in this volume. We have desired to confine ourselves to a study of the more simple and original epitaphs—those which owed their origin to the affection and piety of private individuals, and which only undesignedly threw any light upon the tone of thought and feeling prevalent in the community to which their writers belonged. The inscriptions of Pope Damasus were public monuments set up by authority, and intended *ad perpetuam rei memoriam;* the epitaphs with which we have been concerned were, like those in our own village churchyards, simple chronicles of the dead, each of which, if taken alone, is trifling

Conclusion. 177

enough, but when studied all together, accidentally make interesting and unlooked-for revelations.

We compared them first with Pagan memorials of the same class, and marked their points of difference. We saw that in the beginning these consisted in an omission of what had been usual rather than in the introduction of anything new; that Christian epigraphy, like Christian art in its earliest period, bore close resemblance to the corresponding monuments of Paganism, excepting in those particulars in which the new doctrines either necessarily and at once, or else naturally in the course of time, produced a change. Some of these particulars were not such, perhaps, as we should have expected beforehand, but now that we observe them, we find it easy to account for them; we allude to the disuse of some of the family names, the omission of the names of parents or other survivors who put up the epitaph, the silence as to country, profession and civil *status*, &c. Next we noted the absence of any extravagant outbursts of grief, of murmuring, and rebellion against the dispensations of Providence, and still more remarkably, perhaps, of those retrospects of past enjoyments which are so common on Pagan monuments. We hope we have not given our readers an exaggerated idea of these points of difference; we certainly had no desire to do so. We have studied with close attention several thousands of Pagan epitaphs, and where a little life and display of personal character breaks in on the cold formality which is their general characteristic, we have been as often touched by the voice of nature which speaks in them as shocked by the impiety of their language, or saddened by its frivolity, and still more by its despairing hopelessness. If we have not given such numerous examples of the one class as of the other, this has been because we thought it might be taken for granted.

St. Paul has struck the keynote of the essential difference between Pagan and Christian epitaphs when he bids his Thessalonian converts "not to be sorrowful concerning them that

[side note: Chief characteristic of Christian epitaphs.]

[side note: Their hopefulness.]

M

are asleep, even as others who have no hope." Pagan epitaphs, as we have said, looked back upon the past, and regretted its loss; Christian epitaphs, by the very earliest symbol engraved upon them, spoke the language of hope. If a Pagan mourner dared to look forward at all, it was to utter a feeble wish that he might be allowed to enjoy, as it were, a cold and gloomy repetition, a faint echo or image, of the present life; the Christian prayed for a new and everlasting life in God. The Pagan widow or widower appealed to the Manes that they would put an end to the hateful separation which a cruel fate had made, by bringing about the speedy release of the survivor. A Christian under the same circumstances prayed that the dear departed one might be received among the saints, live with them for ever, and make continual intercession for the one left behind. And this note of difference is to be seen from the very first; the symbols of the dove, the anchor, and the fish, and the acclamations *Vivas in Deo, Vivas inter sanctos*, are found on most certain monuments of primitive Christianity. As time went on, these pious ejaculations were still further developed; and so, step by step, a special style of Christian epigraphy grew up, instinct with the light of hope and faith. This became the generally accepted type, varying indeed, as all things human never fail to vary, in some minor details, according to circumstances of time and place, or the peculiar tastes and fancies of this or that individual, yet sufficiently consistent to set a distinctive mark upon each particular period, whilst by its variations during successive ages it faithfully reflects (we may be sure) some corresponding change in the tone and temper of the ordinary Christian mind.

They reflect contemporary history.   Indeed, it is quite curious to observe how accurately the character of the times is often reflected in Christian epigraphy. Even their secular history leaves its stamp upon it. Thus, when De Rossi has come in the middle of his volume to the year 410, and finds that he has no inscription to record of that year, he exclaims, "Why is this? From the end of the reign of Constantine we have had a continual and sufficiently abundant succession: why is it that for this year a new era, as it were, seems to begin in the history of Roman inscriptions? Now they become more rare; the series goes on with a doubtful, halting step, and very often is altogether stopped; so that in those years which are the nearest to this fatal epoch, there are either very few or absolutely none. Thus, only two or three can be assigned to the year 411 and 412; to the next two years, probably none; from 415 to 418, one for each year perhaps; in 419, three; in 420, probably not one; in 421, certainly none. The cause of this sudden change can only be found in the history of the time. It is evident that this sudden interruption and dearth of monuments portends some great change and disturbance in public affairs." In fact, it is contemporaneous with the attack of Alaric, by which the city suffered almost total ruin, and its records are henceforth marked by sieges, fires, and devastation. Again, at the end of this volume we have another interesting example of this admirable correspondence between the known facts of history and the phenomena presented by the monumental remains that have been preserved to us. He has just registered his last epitaph, belonging to the year 589. "And now," he says, "I seem to be gathering the last relics of the *res epigraphica* of Rome, which had been gradually dying, and indeed was almost dead from about the middle of this (sixth) century. Now I have come to that point where there are no longer even scanty relics to be found; for from the year 589 to the year 600, which is the limit I have prescribed to myself, I can find no Roman epitaph bearing any certain note of its date. The truth is, that during these years the overwhelming calamities of Rome had so passed all limits, that the few citizens who survived for tears and mourning were kept in such a continual state of amazement and distress that their life was more miserable than death. Drowned by inundations of the Tiber, consumed by a terrible pestilence, they had to bear continual attacks from the Lombards during the whole of these ten years; and how great was the misery and destruction they suffered from these evils we can learn from Gregory, truly called The Great, the last of the ancient Romans." After quoting the well-known passages from St. Gregory's Commentary on Ezechiel, he concludes, "These groans of the great St. Gregory from amid the well-nigh empty city still sound in our ears; all the rest is silent, and now even the very graves themselves no longer give forth a voice." He then shows how the same dearth of monuments characterises the next century also, and from the same causes, scarcely more than half-a-dozen monuments bearing dates having been found in Christian Rome for the whole of the seventh century.

And general state of Christian thought and feeling.

Arguing from the same premises, and proceeding with great caution, we cannot help forming some idea as to the general tone of faith and piety among the Christian community at different periods. One may say that nearly the whole of Christian sepulchral epigraphy testifies at least to one Christian doctrine, the doctrine of a future resurrection. *Fiducia Christianorum, resurrectio mortuorum,* says Tertullian, and the language of all the formularies of ancient epitaphs is inspired and impregnated by this confidence. The words *depositus* and *depositio,* instead of *sepultus,* repeated thousands upon thousands of times, proclaims the temporal character of the deposit intrusted to the grave; the words *cœmeterium, dormit, quiescit, jacet in somno, in sopore pacis,* though some of them may have been (very rarely) suggested to Heathen poets by the natural resemblance between death and sleep, yet on Christian gravestones distinctly affirm the same faith, because "on sleeping there follows a wakening and a getting up."[1] Then besides this fundamental doctrine, which can hardly fail to be present to the mind of every Christian under any circumstances when he is consigning the body to the grave,

---

[1] St. Paulinus, Ep. xxxvii. ad Pammachium.

Conclusion. 181

there were in those days of persecution—whilst yet the Christian community was small, all its members most intimately knit together under the pressure of persecution, and with the light of faith shining brightly in their souls, there were—other thoughts of love and hope which rose spontaneously to the heart, and were too strong to be repressed; thoughts of a communion still persisting with the deceased, though now carried on under new conditions, and finding its joy and consolation in incessant mutual prayer. The Pagans at such a moment could only utter a heartrending farewell; to the Christians it rarely occurred to utter that word at all, or, if they did, they accompanied it by some additional phrase which robbed it of its sting of bitterness and desolation, and entirely changed its tone; as, for instance, "Flavius Crispinus to his wife Aurelia Anianes, who lived twenty-eight years, whom I had as a wife for nine years, in love, without any quarrelling" (*lesione animi*),

VALE MIHI KARA IN PACE CUM SPIRITA XANTA VALE IN 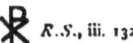 *R.S.*, iii. 132.

"Farewell, my dear one, in peace, with the holy souls.
Farewell in Christ."

In Christ she still lived; in Christ he lived also. In Him, therefore, they were still united, and one could pray for the other.

But in the age of peace, these beautiful formulas, so simple and spontaneous, and so full both of faith and love, were rapidly exchanged for language more or less rhetorical, and other formulas of historical and conventional type. It is scarcely possible to avoid the inference that this change is evidence of a certain depreciation of the general standard of faith and piety amongst the Christians of the fourth and fifth centuries as compared with those of the preceding period. We find amongst the later epitaphs abundant panegyrics of the wisdom, goodness, and innocence of the deceased, but few prayers for his acceptance among the saints. Many widows

At different periods.

and widowers bear testimony to the gentleness and amiability of their consorts, whereby they have been able to live together for long terms of years in perfect harmony, but it does not seem to occur to the survivor to ask for the prayers of the one who has gone before. Children, too, are commended for their innocence and simplicity, but they are not asked to pray for their parents, or for brothers and sisters who survive them; and of the dead generally it is not said that they have gone before in peace, or that they have rendered up their souls to God, or that they have been summoned by Him, or fetched by His angels; neither is it asked that henceforth they may live in God, but the bare record is inscribed upon the stone that they died on such a day, *decessit*, or (in the fifth century and afterwards) that they lie here, *Hic jacet, hic quiescit*, or *requiescit*. Of course, it is not meant that they did not think or feel all these things; but at any rate, the thought and feeling was not so strong and vivid in their minds as to be under any necessity of expression; it did not find vent in the epitaphs.

The general distinction between the two styles of epigraphy, the one before the age of Constantine, the other after it, is a fact of great significance. It is a fact which has only recently been gained to the domain of science by the immense labours and scrupulous accuracy of De Rossi, but it is daily receiving fresh confirmation by the attentive examination of the hundreds of stones which every year brings to light. However, each of these periods is made up of several centuries, and we may confidently expect that the progress of studies and observations will enable us before long to distinguish different groups and families of inscriptions peculiar to each succeeding age. This has already been done in part with reference to the post-Constantinian period, where the number of dated inscriptions makes the work easier. It would be more valuable with reference to the earlier ages; and De Rossi holds out good hopes of our attaining such knowledge by means of the

Conclusion. 183

topographical distinction of the epitaphs, combined with our daily increasing certainty as to the chronology of the several regions of the Catacombs.

It would have been interesting to study the development of Christian epigraphy in other places as compared with Rome; but the materials for such a comparison do not exist. We have been able, indeed, in the preceding pages occasionally to quote a foreign contemporary epitaph in illustration of some Roman monument, but these are rare and valuable exceptions. No country can compete with Rome either in the number or importance of its ancient Christian memorials; and the reason is obvious, because in no other place have they enjoyed so efficient a protection as in the Catacombs. A few have been similarly preserved in Naples, and in the venerable cemetery of the Aliscamps (or Elysian field) at Arles, and in other ancient cemeteries of the valley of the Rhone; and modern scholars are seeking to rescue from oblivion and destruction all the fragments that remain, and by gathering them together into distinct geographical sections, they are doing good service both to church history and to archæology. The most important contribution of this kind has been made in the inscriptions of Gaul by M. Le Blant. It consists of more than 700 examples, but then his chronological limit extends to the end of the seventh century, a hundred years later than De Rossi's, neither is it confined geographically within the present boundaries of his country, but comprehends all regions west of the Rhine and the Alps. From Spain, Hubner has only been able to gather 300, though he extended the limit of time yet another century; and the number collected from our own country by the same scholar is still smaller, even with the addition of some of the ninth and tenth centuries.

Ancient Christian epitaphs in other countries.

If we look to the contents and to the antiquity of these monuments as compared with those of the Roman type, their inferiority becomes still more conspicuous. In Great Britain it is doubtful whether a single specimen can lay claim

Great Britain.

to a date earlier than the sixth century. There is a total absence of the ordinary Christian symbols, such as birds, fish, the anchor, or the palm. Only one or two types of the cross appear. *In pace* is found once (on a stone in the churchyard of Llanerfil, fourteen miles from Welshpool, in Montgomeryshire), *Hic in tumulo jacit Restice filia Paternini an xiii in pa*[*ce*].[1] An equilateral cross, with the upper limb imperfectly shaped into a Rho, so as to give somewhat the appearance of the monogram, and enclosed within a circle, with Alpha and Omega above it, is to be seen in the walls of the burying-ground of Kirkmadrine, on the west side of the bay of Luce, in Wigtownshire, with an inscription which Hubner attributes to the fifth or sixth century, *Hic jacent sci* [*sancti*] *et præcipui sacerdotes, id est Vincentius et Majorius*.[2] And these are really the only points on which the scanty remains of ancient Christianity in this country touch the corresponding monuments in Rome. The favourite British formula was manifestly *Hic in tumulo jacit*, or *Hic jacit*. A large number of the epitaphs begin with these words, and *jacet* is uniformly thus misspelt. The age and the condition of the deceased are rarely recorded.

Spain.

The Christian monuments of Spain present, as might have been expected, more numerous points of resemblance to the ancient Roman type. But these too, with very few exceptions, are of later date than the fifth century. The fish is said to have been found inscribed on the beginning of an inscription not earlier than the latter part of the sixth century; it appears immediately under the monogram, and the deceased, who had lived to the age of seventy-one, is called *famulus Dei*, and is said to have "rested in peace" on such a day, *Acceptâ pœnitentiâ*.[3] The genuineness of this inscription, however, is not altogether free from doubt, and in our own judgment the fish alone is enough to condemn it. In nine or ten epitaphs,

---

[1] Inscript. Brit. Christ., ed. Hubner, No. 125, p. 43.
[2] Ibid., No. 205, p. 74.
[3] Inscript. Hisp. Christ., Hubner, No. 43, p. 13.

Conclusion. 185

belonging to the first quarter of the same century,[1] two doves appear, one on either side of the monogram, to which are generally attached the letters Alpha and Omega. *In hoc tumulo jacet* is sometimes found, but *Recessit in pace* is the formula in most frequent use, and in a few instances either half of this formula stands alone.[2] The length of life or of married life is usually mentioned with considerable accuracy, and the title *famulus Dei* is of frequent recurrence. A few tiles have been found in Spain[3] impressed with the very ancient acclamations, *Marciane vivas in* ☧ *Spes in Deo;* but of course we cannot be certain that these were of native manufacture; and the same must be said of the gold ring found in our own country (at Brancaster, near Norfolk), on which two heads were rudely engraved between the words *Vivas in Deo*.[4]

Gaul.

Among the Christian inscriptions of Gaul there are six bearing date, five of which fall properly within the limits of our inquiry, but they do not make any valuable contribution to our knowledge. The earliest belongs to the year 334, but beyond the date it contains nothing but the words *Depos. Silentiosis.* The second, thirteen years later, is of a priest named Patroclus, *In pace.* ☧ The third, thirty years later still, is not an epitaph, but an inscription testifying to the restoration, on an enlarged scale, of some public building (*longe præstantius illis quæ priscæ steterant*), and it is remarkable as being the most ancient example of the Christian monogram inscribed on a public monument which was not a church. The monogram has the Alpha and Omega on either side of it, and the stone is still preserved in the Hotel de Ville at Sion. The fourth came from the ancient cemetery at Autun. It was "to the eternal memory of a child named Quieta, who only lived one year, three days, and eight hours, and who died (*decessit*) on the 25th of October, A.D. 378." The fifth attests the *depositio* of

L.B., No. 62.

No. 596.

No. 369.

Bull., 1867, p. 25.

L.B., No. 7.

No. 591.

---

[1] Inscript. Hisp. Christ., Hubner, No. 43, p. 13.   [2] P. ix.
[3] P. 66.   [4] Insc. Brit. Christ., p. 81.

186   *Epitaphs of the Catacombs.*

another child named Adelphus, to whom the father and mother inscribed the memorial, A.D. 405. The sixth and last, A.D. 409, is in Greek, and records the burial of a girl aged fifteen, who "lies here in peace," 'ΕΝΘΑ ΚΕΙΤΕ ΕΝ ΕΙΡΙΝΙ.

No. 248.

We must not conclude from the extreme paucity of these dated monuments that all the Christian inscriptions of Gaul are of a later date. We have said that there are more than 700 inscriptions in all, and only about 170 are dated. Their chronology must therefore be determined by other tests; and it seems probable that a few, belonging to the south and southeast, Lyons, Arles, Vienne, and Marseilles, are as old as the third century, many more of the fourth and fifth; and it is announced as the result of very careful observation, that the phrases and symbols used on these ancient epitaphs follow the same chronological order of succession as in Rome, only they begin and end in the province much later than in the metropolis. For instance, the first dated example of the monogram in Gaul, even in its earlier form, is not till the year 377, and in its triumphant form ☧ it is later still. The anchor and the fish are extremely rare, but they are found together in a monument in Marseilles, which bears also another token of great antiquity—viz., the usual termination of Pagan epitaphs, *lib. libertab. posterisque eorum.* Another epitaph in the same place, on which the anchor appears, concludes with one of the ancient Christian acclamations, *Refrigeret nos* . . . At Cimiez, in the department of the Maritime Alps, an epitaph of the year 474 has both the fish and the monogram. The ancient cemetery at Arles, adjoining the church in which, according to local tradition, St. Augustine was consecrated for his mission to England, has given several epitaphs beginning with one of the earliest acclamations, *Pax tecum;* and one of these also is ornamented with an anchor. Doves are met with very frequently, either with the olive branch, or sitting on the edge of a vase, or pecking at grapes, as on the Roman epitaphs; but this was a symbol which was continued even in Rome long after the use of other symbols had dropped, and is no sign

L.B., No. 551 *b.*

No. 584 *a.*

No. 533.

Conclusion. 187

therefore of great antiquity. Once we come across the acclamation *Vale*, not standing alone, however, as on Pagan tombstones, but accompanied by Christian phrases, thus—PAX TECUM IN DEO HAVE VALE. The formula seems to denote a period of transition from Pagan to Christian usage. Christianity had but recently come to the knowledge of the individual who wrote this epitaph, or perhaps it had but recently been introduced to the whole neighbourhood ; and this conjecture is confirmed by finding four or five other epitaphs in the same place, of the most simple and ancient form, the name only, followed by *Pax tecum*. *Vivat in Deo* is the prayer inscribed on the epitaph of a lady who died in the diocese of Rheims at the age of twenty-five, and the epitaph concludes with the familiar words from the fourth Psalm, *In pace dormiam et requiescam ; Vivatis in Deo* is on the epitaph of a double grave, and *Vive Deo* on another stone, found in 1847 in the Cathedral of Le Puy ; but it is doubtful whether this last was really an epitaph, and not rather an acclamation to a Bishop still living (*Scutari papa vive Deo*), like the same legend on a gold ring, found in the Saône, and lately in the possession of Cardinal de Bonald, *Vivas in Deo, Asboli*. [No. 495.] [No. 336 c. No. 576. No. 572.] [No. 29.]

These are the epitaphs in M. Le Blant's collection which reproduce the symbols or acclamations which De Rossi has taught us to be notes of high antiquity, and we see that in Gaul as in Rome their use preceded that of the historical and more prosaic formulæ which make up the bulk of both collections. In both places it is curious to notice how the epitaphs of later date manifest the same tendency to multiply words without any corresponding increase of ideas or of interest. *Hic requiescit* was a formula introduced into Roman epigraphy towards the end of the fourth century. It first appears in Gaul on a stone of the year 422. In 469 we have it with the addition of *in pace ;* in 473 the complimentary epithet of *bonæ memoriæ* makes its appearance, and fifteen years later we get *Hic requiescit in pace bonæ memoriæ*. A few years later still [L.B., i. ix.]

(A.D. 492) we find an additional prefix, or rather an amplification of the old form, *In hoc tumulo requiescit in pace bonæ memoriæ.*

Thus it would seem that in France as in Rome Christian epigraphy manifested a certain tendency to deteriorate from its original simplicity and religious devotional character as time went on. This is not a rash deduction from a limited number of specimens, but a legitimate conclusion drawn from a careful examination of all ascertainable premises. And though we may hope that slow patient industry may yet succeed in recovering many additional materials for the Christian archæologist, both from literary and subterranean researches, and that increased learning may prove equal to the solution of problems which at present baffle his skill, yet the materials already accumulated are so abundant, and the caution and ingenuity exercised upon their combination, comparison, and generalisation has been so great, that we believe there is very little chance of any serious modification of present conclusions being found necessary. We may recover more and more numerous epitaphs of the early Christians in various parts of the world, but we do not doubt that in all cases we shall find greater religious warmth and simplicity to be the characteristics of the most ancient, and that these features were marred and secularised in proportion to the greater extension of the Church, and the consequently greater influx of the ideas and language of the outer world.

INDEX OF GREEK NAMES AND WORDS.

ΑΔΕΛΦΟΙ, 128.
ΑΕΙΜΝΗΣΤΟC, 20, 34.
ΑΙΔΙΑΝΟC, 91.
ΑΝΑΠΑΤCΙC, 83.
ΑΝΔΡΑΓΑΘΟC, 130.
ΑΝΤΕΡΩC, 112.
ΑΤΤΙ ΔΙΚΑ, 49.
ΑΦΡΟΔΙCΙC, 167.
ΑΦΦΙΑΝΟC, 161.
ΑΦΦΙΑΛΑ, 161.

ΓΑΙΟC, 52.
ΓΥΝΗ CΕΜΝΗ, 123.

ΔΗΜΗΤΡΙC, 91.
ΔΙΟΝΥCΙΟC, 94, 117, 130.
ΔΟΥΛΟC ΘΕΟΥ, 91, 104.

ΕΙΡΗΝΗΝ ΕΧΕΤΕ, 128.
ΕΡΓΟΠΟΙΟC, 151.
ΕΤΑΡΕCΤΑ, 101.
ΕΥΤΡΟΠΟC, 171.
ΕΥΤΥΧΙΑΝΟC, 112.

ΖΗCΗC ΕΝ ΘΕΩ, 33.
ΖΩCΙΜΟC, 127.

ΘΕΟCΕΒΗC, 171.
ΘΕΟΦΙΛΟC, 161.

ΙΟΥΛΕΙΑ, 101.
ΙΧΘΥC, 80, 99.

ΚΑΙΚΙΛΙΑΝΟC, 104.
ΚΑΤΑΘΕCΙC, 53, 106.

ΛΕΟΝΤΙΑ, 91.
ΛΟΥΚΙC, 112.

ΜΑΡΤΥΡΙΟΝ, 106.
ΜΑΞΕΙΜΟΥC, 116.
ΜΟΝΑΝΔΡΟC, 123.

ΝΕΟΦΩΤΙCΤΟC, 130.

ΟΞΥΧΟΛΙC, 80.

ΠΑΦΛΑΓΩΝ, 91.
ΠΙCΤΟC, 127.
ΠΡ, 116.
ΠΡΑΙΤΕΞΤΑΤΟC, 104.
ΠΡΩΤΟC, 100.

ΡΟΥΦΙΝΑ, 167.
ΡΩΜΗ, 83.

CΑΒΕΙΝΟC, 21.
CΕΙΡΙΚΑ, 91.
CΕΜΠΡΩΝΙΑ, 123.
CΕΠΤΙΜΙΟC, 104.
CΗΜΕΙΟΝ ΚΥΡΙΑΚΟΝ, 166.
CΩΚΡΑΤΗC, 20.

ΤΙΤΙΑΝΗ, 21.

ΥΓΙΕΙΑ, 33, 35.

ΦΑΒΙΑΝΟC, 112.
ΦΙΛΟΘΕΟC, 20.
ΦΙΛΟΥΜΕΝΗ, 80.
ΦΙΡΜΙΛΛΑ, 100.
ΦΡΟΝΤΩΝ, 104.
ΦΩC ΘΑΝΟΝΤΩΝ, 93.

ΧΑΙΡΕΙΝ ΕΝ ΚΩ, 48.
ΧΡΙCΤΟC ΝΙΚΑ, 167.

INDEX OF LATIN NAMES AND WORDS.

ABUNDANTIA, 18.
Acceptâ pænitentiâ, 184.
Acceptio, 125.
Acceptus apud Deum, 44, 161.
Accersitio, 78.
ADELPHUS, 185.
ADEODATUS, 45.
ADOLIUS (?), 156.
Ædificia Manium, 26.
ÆLIUS, 156.
ÆSTONIA, 80.
AFRODITE, 144.
AGAPE, 80.
AGATOPUS, 106.
Agnellus Dei, 33.
ALEXANDER, 172.
ALEXANDRA, 121.
Alumna, 93.
Alumnus, 107, 150.
AMANTIUS, 45.
Amator pauperum, 145.
AMERIMNUS, 80.
AMIAS, 100.
ANASTASIUS, 45.
ANATOLIUS, 80, 156.
Ancilla Dei et Christi, 121.
Anima dulcis, 107, 121.
—— *mellita*, 175.
ANTISSIUS, 156.
ANTONIA, 156.
APOLLINARIS, 156.
APRILIS, 156.
Arcessitus ab angelis, 44.
Aromatarius, 146.
ASCLEPIODOTUS, 161.
ASELLUS, 156.
ASTERIUS, 107.
ATENAGORAS, 122.
ATTICIANUS, 120.
ATTICUS, 88, 99.
Ave, 60, 187.
AUGURINUS, 99.
AURELIUS AGAPETUS, 93.
—— ANIANES, 181.
—— CASTUS, 156.

AURELIUS PROBUS, 156.
—— SCOLACIUS, 142.
AUXENTIA, 142.

BACCIS, 121.
BACIUS, 80.
BASSILLA, 80, 107.
BAUDILIUS, 107.
BAUTO, 156.
BENEDICTUS, 94.
Benemerenti, 68.
BENEROSUS, 92.
BENIGNUS, 150.
BICTORINA, 80.
Sine bile, 69, 85.
Bimus, 131.
B.M., 30.
B.N.M., 95.
BOLOSA, 80.
Bona fœmina, 152.
Bonæ memoriæ, 30, 47, 119, 187.
In bono, 88.
BONOSUS, 45.

CAIUS, 57.
CAPRIOLE, 175.
Carus suis, 69.
CASSIA, 144.
CASTOR, 80.
CASTUS, 156.
CELERINA, 156.
CELERINUS, 31.
CELSINIANUS, 93.
CERVONIA, 123.
CHRESIMUS, 82.
CHRISTUS *verus*, 94.
CIMITERIUM, 107, 180.
CŒMETERIUM OSTRIANUM, 35.
Cognomina diacritica, 35.
Consecutio, 126.
Consequi, 125, 131.
Conservantia, 31.
Consignatus, 131.
CONSTANTIA, 150.
Constitutus fide, 125.

Index of Latin Names and Words.

CONTUMELIOSUS, 45.
CORNELIUS, 105.
CORYTUS, 144.
CRESCENS, 156.
CRESCENTIANUS, 156.
CRESCENTINUS, 80.
Credidit in unu Deu, 98, 103.
CRISPINUS, 181.

DAFNEN, 80.
DAMASUS EPISCOPUS, 113.
Dece, 22.
Decedere, 80.
Deceperunt, 72.
Depositio, 41, 79, 180.
Devoti Sanctis, 108.
DEUSDEDIT, 45.
DEUS UNUS, 98, 103.
DIES DOMINICA, 28.
DI MANES, 58.
Dies Marturorum, 107.
D.M., 22.
D.J.M., 24.
DIONYSIUS, 174.

D.M. ☧ S., 99.
D.O.M., 24.
DOMNUS, 57, 106, 107.
Domus æterna, 30, 76.
Dormit, 47, 180.
D.P., 79.
Dulciaria, 146.
Dulcis anima, 107, 121.
Dulcissimus, 34, 68.

Elatus, 72.
ELIS, 156.
ELPIS, 33, 156.
EPICTETUS, 156.
EUTYCHIANES, 163.
EVOCHIAS, 101.
EUODIUS, 108.
Exire de sæculo, 80.

Famulus Dei, 122, 184.
FAVOR, 120.
FASCIOLÆ TITULUS, 120.
FAUSTINA, 80, 99.
FAUSTINIANI, 147.
FAUSTINIANUS, 164.
FAUSTINUS, 99.
Fecit bene, 149.
FELICISSIMUS, 106.
FELICITAS, 33, 93.
FELIX, 156.
Fidelis, 109, 125.
Fidem accipere, 125.
FILUMENA, 33, 34.
FLAVIUS SABINUS, 21.

FLORENTIUS, 33, 144, 156.
FONS BETHLEMICUS, 135.
FORTUNATA, 34.
FORTUNIO, 141.
FRATRES, 95, 127.
FRATRES ARVALES, 129.
FREDA, 49.
Fuisti, 60.

GEMELLUS, 80.
GENIALIS, 156.
GENTIANUS, 109.
Gravare ecclesiam, 80, 125.

HELIODORUS, 116.
Hic jacet, hic quiescit, &c., 43, 182.
Hic requiescit in somno pacis, 48.
Hic situs est, 48.
Homo Dei, 102, 122.

Illuminare, 129.
Infantes, 130.
Inlibata, 124.
Innocens, 35, 67.
Innocentium misericors, 31.
INOFITUS, 80.
IPOLITUS, 106.
IRENE, 167.

JANUARIA, 94.
JANUARIUS, 106.
JOVINA, 57.
JOVIANUS, 94.
JULIANUS, 101.
JUNIANUS, 145.

KYRIACUS, 80, 101.

Laborum auctrix, 151.
LATINILLA, 119.
LATINUS, 119.
LAURENTIUS, 106.
LECTOR, 119.
LEO, 156, 175.
LEONTIUS, 45, 128.
LEOPARDUS, 23, 80, 120.
Sine lesione animi, 69.
LEUCES, 19.
LEX DEI, 98.
LIBERIUS PAPA, 111.
LINUS, 110.
LIVIA, 164.
LOLLIUS, 60.
LUCIFERA, 95.
LUCILIANUS, 80.
LUCIUS, 102.

MACRINUS, 119.
MÆCIUS, 156.

MAJORIUS, 184.
MARCELLINA, 80.
MARCELLINUS, 108.
MARCIA, 142.
MARTYRIUS, 45.
MATRONATA MATRONA, 80.
MAXIMA, 156.
MENSURIUS, 98.
MICINA, 80.
MINISTRATOR CHRISTIANUS, 117.
Miræ bonitatis, 153.
M.M., 95.

NATALE, 55, 107, 118.
NAVIRA, 175.
NEOPHYTUS, 80.
NICARUS, 164.
NICEN, 59.
In Nomine Dei, 98.
NOTATUS, 141.
Nove, 22.
Nutricatus Deo, Christo et Martyribus, 108.

ONAGER, 175.
Operaria, 145, 150.
Sine offensa, 69.

Palumbo sine felle, 152.
In pace, 30, 75, 86.
In pacem, 23.
PAPA LIBERIUS, 111-115.
PARTHENIUS, 23.
PASCHASIUS, 45.
Passionis dies, 107.
PASTOR, 80.
PATERNINUS, 184.
PATROCLUS, 185.
PAULINA, 119.
PAULINUS, 80.
PAULUS, 25, 90, 100, 119.
Pax a fratribus, 128.
Pax ecclesiæ, 48.
Pax tibi, 33, 74.
Pax tecum, 33, 74, 187.
PECORIS, 107.
PEREGRINUS, 49, 80.
Pete pro parentibus, 41.
Petitus in pace, 44.
PETRONIA, 142.
PETRUS, 100.
PHILOMUSUS, 175.
PHILUMENA, 33.
PHŒBE, 93.
PIE ZESES, 44.
Pius in suos, 69.
PONTIA, 156.
PONTIUS, 122, 156.
PORCELLA, 156.

P.P., 95, 115.
Præcedere, præmitti, 78.
Præpositus, 113.
Præstator pauperum, 145.
PRETIOSA, 121.
PRIMA, 89.
PRIMUS, 119.
PROBA, 156.
PROBILIANUS, 151.
PROJECTUS, 92.
P.T.N, 95.
Puer, 130.
Puer reverentissimus, 66.
Pueri Faustiniani, 147.

Q.D., 95.
Sine quereld, 69.
QUIETUS, 185.
QUINCTILIANUS, 102.
QUODVULT DEUS, 45.

Recedere, 78, 80.
Receptus ad Deum, 44, 75, 141.
RECTOR, 115.
Reddidit spiritum, 23, 94.
REDEMPTUS, 45.
Refrigeret, 41, 106, 123.
Refrigerium, 78.
REFRIGERIUS, 45.
REGINA, 80, 125.
REGIO SECUNDA, 120.
Religio Dei, 98.
RENATUS, 45.
RESTICE, 184.
Retro sanctos, 106.
ROMANUS, 118.
RUFINA, 31, 80, 142.

SABBATIA, 162.
SABBATIUS, 94.
SABINUS, 156.
Sacerdos, 115.
SALONICE, 88.
Salve, 60.
SILVA, 60.
Salvo Episcopo, 113.
SAVINIANUS, 88.
Inter sanctos, 89.
SCOLACIUS, 142.
Scrupulus, 27.
SCUTARIUS, 187.
SECUNDA, 152.
Sedente Liberio, 112.
Septe, 22.
SEVERA, 19.
Signum, 35, 175.
SILENTIOSUS, 185.
SILVANA, 123.
SILVANUS, 90.

Sit tibi terra levis, 61.
SOTERIS, 107.
SOZON, 94.
SPERANTIA, 156.
SPES, 33.
Spirita sancta, 23, 25, 41, 123, 181.
Spiritus Sanctus, 19, 101.
STATILIA, 121.
STERCORIUS, 28.
S.T.T.L., 61.
Sine stomacho, 69.
Sub Damaso, 113.
Summitas, 103.
Suscipiant, 25, 90, 108.
SYNTROPHION, 132.

Tituli Fasciolæ, 120.
—— *Vestinæ*, 118.
Trimus, 131.
TYRANIUS, 167.

ULPIA, 128.
ULPIANI, 147.
Unibyra, 125.
Univira, 70, 123.
Unus Deus, 98.
URANIA, 33.

Vale, 60, 128, 181, 187.
VALERIUS, 80.
VENERA, 92.
VERONICE, 33.
VERUS, 116.
Verus Christus, 94.
VESTINUS, 144.
Via Nova, 174.
VICTORIA, 122, 145, 156.
VICTORINA, 34, 80, 156.
Vidua Dei, 124.
VINCENTIUS, 45, 93, 184.
VIRGINIUS, 93, 123.
Virgo, 80.
Virgo Dei, 123.
VITALIS, 80.
Vivas cum fratribus tuis, 128.
—— *in Deo*, 41, 47, 80, 185.
—— *in Spirito Sancto*, 80.
—— *inter sanctos*, 44.
Vixit in pace, 48.
Vocabulum, 35.

YACINTHUS, 106.

ZESUS, 80.
ZOSIMUS, 156.

INDEX OF ENGLISH NAMES AND WORDS.

ABERCIUS, epitaph of, 134.
Abraham's bosom, 90.
Acolytes, tombstones of, 118.
Acts of Martyrs, 84, 139.
Ad such and such a saint, 55.
Affection, expressions of, on Pagan epitaphs, 64.
African inscriptions, 48, 120, 128.
Agathopus, a favourite Christian name, 166.
Age, minutely measured, 26; measured from baptism, 126.
Alcuin's scholars collect Christian inscriptions, 10.
Allusions to dogma in epitaphs, 97 *et seq.*
Alpha and Omega, 30, 85.
Alumni, condition of, 142; epitaphs of, 44, 108.
Anchor, very ancient emblem, 32, 33, 74, 82, 126, 162.
Angels, 105.
Anointing used for confirmation, 130.
Arrangement of inscriptions should be topographical, 14; in the Lateran Museum, 8; in De Rossi's work, 15.
Astrology, traces of, 27.
Augustine, St., treatise *de Curâ pro Mortuis*, 106.
Autun, epitaph at, 135.

BAKER, symbol of, 171.
Baptism, 130.
Baptistery of St. Peter's, 32.
Basilicas in cemeteries, 38.
Belief in one God, 98.
Benemerenti, 68.
Bernardin de St. Pierre quoted, 138.
Blacksmith, symbols of, 151, 170.
B.M., 23.
Bishop, title when used, 110.
Bosio's collection of epitaphs from Catacombs, 12.

Blunders in interpreting epitaphs, 137.
Bread and fish on monuments, symbol of the Holy Eucharist, 133.
Brethren, why Christians so called, 129.
Burial service, 90.

CAIUS, Pope, his epitaph, 50-53.
Calabrian epitaph, 101.
Carpenter, symbols of, 156, 170.
Catechumen, 130.
Caution required in interpreting epitaphs, 137.
Cemeteries, 79; above ground, 38.
Charity, Christian, 129, 144.
Children exposed by Pagan parents, 143; praises of, 31, 66, 151.
Christ, belief in, 99.
Chronology of inscriptions, 35-47.
Confirmation, sacrament of, 130.
Constantinian monogram, 168.
Corn-dealer, symbol of, 171.
Cornelius, Pope, epitaph of, 105.
Cross, various forms of, 166-170.
Crowns, symbols of victory, 165.
Crux gammata, 167.
Cyprian's, St., instruction on death, 77; called Pope, 115.

DAMASUS' prayers to the saints, 96; inscriptions, 176.
Dated inscriptions, 37.
Day of death or burial recorded, 31, 38.
Days of the week, Heathen names of, 27.
Deacons, epitaphs of, 117.
Death to a Pagan without hope, 59, 72.
Debtor to God, 86.
Dentist, symbol of, 172.

Index of English Names and Words. 195

De Rossi's arrangement of inscriptions in Lapidarian Gallery, 8; collection of Christian inscriptions, 13.
—— method of fixing chronology, 39.
D.M. explained, 22.
Dove with olive branch or palm, 23, 32, 82, 161, 171, 186.
Dulcis, 68.

EPITAPHS, universally used, 1; their characteristics, 2; interest, 2, 138; purpose, 2; spurious, 25; facetious or malicious, 61.
—— ancient Christian, in Rome, their number, 3; history of their destruction, 4; their dispersion, their characteristics, 177; collections of, 6.
—— to husbands and wives, 151.
—— to children, 152; manner of writing, 18, 43; reflect contemporary history, 179; and state of Christian thought, 180.
—— Pagan, their characteristics, 58-67; to husbands and wives, 67; to children, 64.
Eternal sleep, 76, 81.
Eucharist, Holy, represented under symbols, 133-135.
Exorcists, tombstones of, 119.

FAITH, called the mother of Christians, 135, 140; given in baptism, 125.
Feast, symbol of joys of heaven, 85.
Filocalus, Furius Dionysius, 114.
Fish, ancient emblem, 23, 32, 126, 132; and anchor, 165; and bread, 132-136; of the living, 100.
Fisherman, symbols of, 151, 170.
Flavii, 45.
Fossors probably reckoned with *ostiarii*, 120.
Fratres, the title of Christians, 128.
Fratres Arvales, 129.
Freedmen rarely mentioned on Christian epitaphs, 141; epitaph of one to another, 71.

GEOGRAPHICAL differences of inscriptions, 47.
Gnostics, 49, 130.
Good, in, 88.
Grave an everlasting home, 76.
Greek language on Roman epitaphs a sign of antiquity, 21, 41.

"HATRED of the human race" charged against Christians, 153.
Heaven, joys of, represented as feast, 85.
Hebrew language used once in Catacombs, 21.
Hierapolis, ancient church of, 134.
Holy Ghost, belief in, 47, 100.
Hope characteristic of Christian epitaphs, 177.
"Hope of future resurrection," 49, 180.
Horse as a Christian emblem, 166.
Hubner's collection of Christian inscriptions in Britain, 183; Spain, 184.
Husbands, praises of, 67.

INNOCENCE, praises of, 151.
Inscriptions, Christian, copied by Alcuin's scholars, 10; scratched in mortar, 18; of Ostia, 32, 47; of Porto, 47; two great classes, 41.
Institutions, Pagan, for children, 147.
Intercession of the saints, 108.
Ispiritus for *spiritus*, 22.

JUVENAL'S character of Roman ladies, 67.

LABOUR, Christian estimate of, 151.
Languages mixed on Pagan inscriptions, 21; Christian inscriptions, 19; Greek, use of, 21, 41.
Lapidarian Gallery, history of, 6-8.
Latin words written in Greek, 19.
Laudatory epithets, 31.
Le Blant quoted, 49, 183.
Lectors, epitaphs of, 120.
Length of life minutely measured, 26.
Liberius, Pope, 113.
Liberti, 142.
Life, different views of, on Pagan epitaphs, 62-64.
Life in God, 24, 82, 84.
—— counted from baptism, 126.
—— prayer for, 84, 92.
Light, prayers for, 91.
Light of the dead, 92.
Lighthouse and ship, meaning of, 165.
Liturgies, ancient, 86.
Love of labour, 150.
—— of the poor, 145.
Lyons, 48.

MANES, prayers to, 24, 26, 60, 71.
Marriage, age of, 121.
Martyrs, title of, 105; burial near, 106; invoked, 106.
M'Caul, Dr., 24.
Mass, prayers for the dead in, 90.
Merivale, Dr., quoted, 20, 61.
Medals of St. Laurence, 108.
Mommsen quoted, 39.
Monogram of name of Christ, 168.
—— with D.M., 23, 30.
Museum, Lateran, history of, 8.

NAMES, number of, 35, 45, 154.
—— peculiar to Christians, 45.
Natural affection among Romans, 64.
Neophyte, 129.
Noetus, 99.

Orante, 23.
Osiris invoked to give cold water to the dead, 86.
Ostia, 32, 47.
Ostiarii, number of, 119.

Pace, in, 30, 86.
Painted inscriptions, 32.
Palm branch, 32, 74.
Pancrazio, St., 32.
Patripassians, 99.
Patronus, 108.
Paulinus of Nola, 86, 90.
Peace, meaning of, 86.
Peacock, meaning of, 164.
Perpetua, St., Acts of, 85.
Pestilence in Africa, 77.
Peter and Paul, SS., their portraits on epitaphs, 170.
Pity, view of, among Pagans, 148.
Pliny's charitable institution for children, 147; portraits of Roman ladies, 67.
Pomponio Leto, 11.
Pope, title of, 115.
Popes, epitaphs of, 112.
Porto, 47.
Prayers for the dead, 81-93.
—— to the saints, 93-96.

Presbyter, 117.
Priscilla, St., 32.
Puer, 130.

RAOUL-ROCHETTE, 24.
Refreshment, prayers for, 85.
Resignation, want of, 64.
Resurrection, expectation of, 47, 180; the first, 89.

SABELLIANS, cemetery of, 102.
Sabinus, Peter, first collector of Christian inscriptions, 11.
Sarcophagi, maker of, 171.
Salutations on Pagan tombstones, 60.
Sculptor, symbols of, 151, 170.
Seneca's view of pity and beneficence, 148.
Sententiæ sepulchrales, 62.
Severus the deacon, his epitaph, 46.
Shepherd, the Good, 155.
Ship, ancient Christian symbol, 82, 133, 165.
Sleep for death, 23, 79, 180.
Sicilian inscriptions, 127.
Slaves, no mention of, on Christian epitaphs, 140; emancipated by Christians, 142.
Soldiers, epitaphs of, 174.
Soteris, St., 55.
Spanish inscriptions, 69, 122.
Spelling, corrupt forms of, 21.
Subdeacon, 118.
Summitas used for God, 104.
Symbols, ancient, 41; religious, 155; civil, 170; nominal, 174.

T (Tau), a form of the cross, 167.

VIRGIN, the Blessed, 135.
Virgins, epitaphs to, 121.
Virtues, domestic, of Roman women, 69.

WIDOWS, epitaphs of, 124.
Wives, praises of, 24, 70.
Women, praises of, 69.

www.ingramcontent.com/pod-product-compliance
Lightning Source LLC
Chambersburg PA
CBHW020914230426
43666CB00008B/1447